Jeffy's Journal
Raising a Morgan Horse

Janet Wilder Dakin

The Stephen Greene Press/Pelham Books

THE STEPHEN GREENE PRESS/PELHAM BOOKS

Published by the Penguin Group
Viking Penguin, a division of Penguin Books USA Inc., 375 Hudson
Street, New York, New York 10014, U.S.A.
Penguin Books Ltd., 27 Wrights Lane, London W8 5TZ, England
Penguin Books Australia Ltd., Ringwood, Victoria, Australia
Penguin Books Canada Ltd., 2801 John Street, Markham, Ontario,
Canada L3R 1B4
Penguin Books (N.Z.) Ltd., 182-190 Wairau Road, Auckland 10,
New Zealand

Penguin Books Ltd., Registered Offices: Harmondsworth, Middlesex,
England

First published in 1990 by The Stephen Greene Press/Pelham Books
Distributed by Viking Penguin, a division of Penguin Books USA Inc.

10 9 8 7 6 5 4 3 2 1

The contents of this book were first published as Janet Dakin's column,
"Jeffy's Journal" in the magazine *The Morgan Horse* and are reprinted by
permission of the publisher.
Photographs from the author's collection.

Library of Congress Cataloging-in-Publication Data
Dakin, Janet Wilder.
    Jeffy's journal: raising a Morgan horse / by Janet Wilder Dakin;
edited by Sheila Rainford.
        p.   cm.
    ISBN 0-8289-0767-6
    1. Morgan horse—Biography.   2. Dakin, Janet Wilder.
I. Rainford, Sheila.   II. Title.
SF293.M8D34   1990
636.1'7—dc20   89-25649
                                                                    CIP

Printed in the United States of America
Set in Palatino by Compset, Inc.
Designed by Kenneth J. Wilson
Produced by Unicorn Production Services, Inc.

To my mother,
Isabel Thornton Niven Wilder

ACKNOWLEDGMENTS

I WISH to thank everyone who helped me publish this book. Special thanks to Marge Davenport, who spent long hours typing the manuscript, and to the fine photographers who took such beautiful photos of Jeffy. I tried to contact you all, but some are unknown by both the post office and the Morgan Horse Association. Special thanks to photographers Ira Haas and William Freudy whom I was unable to contact.

Very special thanks to Sheila Rainford for her services as editor, agent, and friend.

CONTENTS

PREFACE

WHEN Janet Wilder Dakin published *Jeffy's Journal* as a series in *The Morgan Horse* from December 1952 through April 1956, readers responded with delight and letters of appreciation. I know, because I was one of those readers. At that time I was a schoolgirl very much in love with horses, especially Morgans, but I had not yet met Janet Dakin. Now, of course, I am somewhat older and have had time and opportunity to meet and know Janet. When I recently ran across her manuscript of *Jeffy's Journal* and read through it, I was enthralled all over again. *Jeffy's Journal* is a truly timeless record of experiences shared by Janet and her Morgan foal, Lord Jeff.

Janet was reluctantly introduced to horses when she was a schoolgirl. Because she was sickly, her doctor suggested that she take up riding to improve her health. She didn't want to ride, but her mother wisely insisted that she do so. Once enrolled in an excellent riding school in Oxford, England, she quickly fell deeply and permanently in love with horses.

Although Janet received high-quality riding instruction in England when she was a girl and continued to ride, own horses, and be an active member of horse associations, she was still completely inexperienced in raising a foal when Jeffy was born. With her adventuresome nature and light-hearted good spirit, she set out to teach Jeffy as much as she could with little experienced help and no major accidents or injuries either to herself or to Jeffy. Because she owned only Jeffy and his mother, she was able to meet her goals of taking care of them entirely by herself, giving them much individual attention, and accurately recording her observations in a carefully kept journal.

As Janet's enthusiasm for raising a foal increased, she decided to share her journal with readers of *The Morgan Horse*. Energetic and organized as she is, she couldn't simply reproduce the journal. Instead, using the journal as a base, she carefully crafted a series of articles focused on topics of interest to beginners and owners of only one or two horses. In these articles she outlines her training methods, describes her feelings, discusses problems, and even owns up to her mistakes.

Any lover or owner of horses should find this journal both fun to read and helpful. It is filled with anecdotes containing practical, ageless information that can help the novice horse owner avoid pitfalls and the experienced horseperson recall with a smile many personal adventures involving bright, energetic horses. I hope you will enjoy reading *Jeffy's Journal* as much as I have.

Sheila Rainford

CHAPTER 1

The Birth

THE week before Jeffy's birth was a period of beautiful, clear, soft starlit nights. Never have I seen such lovely nights, but never have I had the opportunity to study them for a week at three o'clock in the morning. It is a rewarding experience to be alone in a pasture with your mare when all the world appears to sleep. My purpose in being there at that hour was to see if she needed help in foaling or to bring them both in if she had foaled. Shortly before my three o'clock visit on June 15, 1952, Jeffy was born, just 343 days after Bonnie's breeding.

Everybody rallies around to help with your first foal. Some come by invitation and a good many come just to have a share in the business. You will be deluged with advice, and your mare will be subjected to the most intimate scrutiny. Bonnie had been slow to show her condition, so the consensus of these friends was that Bonnie was not in foal. This was in March. I called the great Doc. "Yes," he said, "she is pregnant although she does not show it." We then built the big foaling stall by removing the partition between her box stall and the adjoining straight stall. With all this unusual space to roll in, she did so with abandon and one night became cast. The long horizontal scratch marks and shoe imprints on the broken-out Dutch door showed me what had happened. She was loose in the pasture that morning.

All fall and winter I had been riding her regularly, but quietly, and by the spring with increasing caution. Toward the end we were no fun to ride with and so we went out alone.

1

This carefulness was probably quite unnecessary but that is the way I am. As spring progressed she became more sluggish. I took to riding bareback, so that at least I could improve my seat as we walked and jogged around the neighborhood. By the first of June I gave up even that and wondered why I had thought it would be fun to have a foal. It was a tiresome period. I am sure that mares are not always so lethargic. Bonnie is a highly conservative creature and broodiness just comes naturally to her.

The doctor had advised that she be allowed to foal either in her stall or out at pasture, whichever she preferred. Mares had an easier time foaling if they could do it where they wanted to, so he said. Therefore, from the middle of May on her stall door was fastened open and she was free to come and go, night and day, between stall and pasture. I disinfected her stall by washing the walls and sloshing the floor with Lysol and made her a deep bed of bright, long straw. According to the advice in my many books I filled a basket with clean towels, iodine, disinfectant, scissors, and string. By now you are saying what a worrywart I am. True enough, I am one. However, any big stable of valuable horses takes these and other precautions. I see no reason why the single mare in the amateur barn should not have as good attention as is allowed by time and manpower, whatever her value. There is also a tendency to scorn books in practical matters. To that I say that the knowledge found in books can do much to make up for the lack of experience, and it can also correct "helpful" advice. Most of the writers, although not all of them, know what they are talking about; and if they communicate it intelligibly they can be a very real help.

Before the first of June, wax formed on Bonnie's nipples. Foaling could be any time. Soon after June 1, milk started to flow. She could foal any day then. Day after day passed. She dozed almost all day just inside the box stall door with her head hanging to her knees. At night she would wander out to pasture with slow and stately tread to graze. These were trying days.

On June 11 the milk sprayed out in a small mist hitting the ground with a slight, rhythmic hiss as she walked, grazing.

2

She should foal by morning. June 12, 13, and 14 were the same. According to her symptoms she was long overdue. I had developed a schedule for observation at about eleven at night, three in the morning, and at six. At any time my husband, Toby, and I expected to find that we had two horses in the pasture. On June 14 she seemed livelier. She walked around in the daytime and reacted pleasantly to my attentions.

Three o'clock in the morning, June 15, found me drugged with sleep on the way to the barn. A soft, low mutter was a new night sound. It was Bonnie beside herself in an ecstasy of joy, licking and talking to the perfect little foal who lay in the straw, its little head waving like a blossom on its stalk. Bonnie did not mind at all when I came into the stall to help dry her baby. It struggled to rise and fell back. I saw that it was still attached to the placenta, which lay in a neat heap beside it on the straw. I let it struggle for a while thinking the cord would break and free it from the heavy anchor of the afterbirth. Both Bonnie and I became concerned, and so I dipped some string in iodine, tied the cord, cut it, and applied more iodine. Then Jeffy was free to rise. He got up on long wavering legs. Bonnie watched with amazement in a way that seemed to say "Great Scot, what's this?" She retreated, rolling her eyes and snorting with astonishment. Jeffy on the other hand knew what he wanted and just where to find it. He chased her three times around the stall in long weaving staggers. I tried to hold her once but just increased her nervousness, and so I got right out of the way. All the time I could almost see Bonnie listening to some inner voice that was trying to tell her that all was well. Finally she stood still in a corner and let Jeffy nurse, though she screamed when he did it.

Jeffy was from the first a vigorous, sturdy little colt. How did Bonnie make out in this great adventure? When I saw her almost immediately after foaling, she was as dry as a bone and as clean as a whistle, up on her feet, and livelier than I had seen her in many days. She apparently had not had the least bit of trouble. She was as happy as a mare can be with her first foal.

3

Jeffy, at two days old, likes to be
in the pasture with his mother.

Jeffy, at seven days old, stands
next to Bonnie, June 22, 1952.

Jeffy relaxes in the pasture. He
is twelve days old.

Jeffy enters the National Morgan Horse Show as a foal, August 1952.

CHAPTER 2

First Lessons

JEFFY was four months old on October 15. This month we concentrated on two things: the outside world of traffic, dogs, and other horses and how to stand quietly tied up. Because Jeffy's barn and pasture are so far from the road that he sees and hears no traffic in his daily living, we have to go out to it. At first Toby led Bonnie out to the roadside and let her graze. I led Jeffy and had to dig my heels in and hang on when a car went by. Soon he paid little attention to the passing cars. I then took him out alone almost every day for a little while. This month I led him from Bonnie's back. We only go about a mile, slowly, but we take in as much traffic as we can in that distance and then go through a rather rough and hilly orchard for practice in rough footing. Jeffy's own small pasture is almost too smooth and level.

Before we went out at all this way, Jeffy knew that "whoa" meant to stop right away and stay stopped. He had been perfect on that for at least a month. "Whoa" followed in a second or two by a sharp jerk on the halter lead line teaches that easily. Both "no" and "walk" sound too much like "whoa," so I say "bad" to accompany punishment and "steady" as he jogs.

When I lead him from horseback he must stay beside my right knee. I leave his head entirely free unless I have to jerk him up when he lags or give an admonitory tug if he goes ahead. The lead line is a nine-foot length of webbing. I do not believe in ropes longer than a tie rope near a horse because of possible rope burns. The greater length passes under the palm of my left hand on top of the reins and hangs down Bonnie's near shoulder; it is just there in case of need. My right hand holds the line to Jeffy's head and keeps it away from my foot to avoid a tangle. Thus we went out six times with no trouble at all. If, however, Bonnie were a nervous, jittery mare this might well be worse than useless because Jeffy copies her attitudes and what she does.

I tie him up for a little while several times a week. Since he was a week old I have tied him for a few minutes while I groom him. In the early days I tied him up when just fooling around was more fun than eating. To tie him to the manger seemed to encourage his eating because there was nothing else to do. I made the mistake once of using a neck rope, fortunately of soft cotton, without a halter. I left him to get some hay, and when I came back I found him lying back on the rope gasping for breath. He had worked the loop around so the bight came out between his ears, instead of under his chin, and he was choking. Before I could get to him, he had slipped it off and was free. He had scared and hurt himself and he had learned what I had hoped he never would—that he could get free when tied. So this month I tie him for longer and longer periods using the cotton neck rope with the free end run through the center ring of his halter so he can't work it into a choking position. He has never pulled back again. I hope he gets another futile pullback off his mind now while he is both safely and securely tied.

So far Jeffy is a good little boy and no problem. My friends who have had other breeds of colts say "Just you wait." He kicked a few times before he was a month old—a single quick smack on the buttock and "bad" seems to have stopped that. He has never yet struck out with a foreleg. He does nip, but I think he is learning not to. Of course I realize that I have started very young with him, but while he is small enough for me to handle alone I want to eliminate the little incidental problems that can cause trouble and complicate his more advanced training when he is older and stronger.

CHAPTER 3

My Horses and
How They Live

LITTLE has happened in Jeffy's life of late so it is a good time to describe him and Bonnie, his dam, and how they live.

Jeffy is bay with black legs and a black mane and tail. He has a small white star, a little off center, on his forehead. It is too early, I think, to say much about his temperament except that he is sociable and a good-natured but spunky little creature. Bonnie is a very dark chestnut with a star, strip, and snip. I bought her just before her third birthday. She is now six years old. Jeffy is her first foal. Her disposition now, as an adult, is the product of her heredity and her environment and her relations with man. Her dominant characteristic might be called serenity. She is amiable toward people but a little aloof and independent. She displays jealousy if Jeffy gets too much attention. Of course when her foal is taken from her, her serenity is upset and she calls and appears to worry. However, I usually find she has eaten quite a bit of hay when I bring him back, so her anxiety is not too severe. Jeffy's sire is a very well known stud, with an impressive record both in model and performance classes in shows. He has an excellent disposition, style, animation, and presence—all characteristics I hope Jeffy inherits in part at least.

How do these two horses, Bonnie and Jeffy, live? Their barn is the south end of a cinder-block rectangular building.

Bonnie at
three years of age, just
after I bought her, 1949.

Bonnie is curious but serene
when some noisy geese come to
my field.

The north end is the garage. At present, since Jeffy is not yet five months old, they share one stall. It is eleven by fifteen feet and was made for Bonnie's foaling by throwing together her box stall and an adjacent straight stall. It has a dirt floor, five-foot walls made of oak, and two doors. One opens onto the cement aisle; the other, a Dutch door, opens into a small paddock, about fifty by seventy feet, to the west. The paddock in turn opens into a small pasture of about one acre. Most of the time the horses are free to come and go between stall and pasture both day and night. This arrangement has one serious fault. Our prevailing winter winds are from the northwest, and our land is so situated that not even one tree blocks the force of this wind for a distance of at least fifteen miles. It sweeps right across the Connecticut Valley, over the pasture, and into the stall if the door is open. A lesser fault is that the pasture is too small for mare and foal. It was planned to provide grass (as a dietary supplement) and a place to exercise for a single horse. Both paddock and pasture are surrounded by a five-foot cedar rail fence. There is no wire anywhere to be a danger to the horses. Now, in November, they are shut in at night because of the wind.

Both horses get grained twice a day, morning and late afternoon. I learned as a child that horses should be fed at very regular times, that they keep in better condition that way. So I choose the times best suited in general to my life, and I stick to them, even when I have to hire Billy (the boy down the street) for the late afternoon feeding because I will be delayed a couple of hours away from home. They have water available at all times. Bonnie likes to dunk her hay, and Jeffy is beginning to copy her. At first he didn't get the idea; he would take a mouthful and hold it over the water pail. A few days ago I saw him dip it in the water. Bonnie really sloshes it around. This makes an awful mess in the pail but is good because it lays the dust on the hay. Hay is available for them on the floor most of the time. They get groomed four or five times a week. This is a lapse from my earlier standard, but now that I am not using Bonnie they are being partly "roughed." The stall is cleaned twice daily with varying degrees of thoroughness.

Bonnie and Jeffy's stable as seen from the paddock. The north end of the building is the garage.

People who don't have horses sometimes ask how much time and how much work is needed. Apart from exercise, I estimate that a rapid worker spends about an hour a day, divided into about three periods, taking care of one pleasure horse. This includes a minimum sort of grooming, cleaning the stall, feeding, and other routine basic care. Now and then the stall needs a good clean-out, tack needs to be cleaned, and special attentions given the horse. So much for time spent on a single family horse, not a show horse.

As for work, a horse will give you between thirty and forty pounds of manure and soiled bedding to haul off each day, and even minimum grooming is pretty strenuous. The work can be added to the credit side for people who lead a sedentary life.

A horse should get out a part of every day all year round, either loose in an enclosure or under saddle or in harness. Exercise is something to be planned for before purchase.

CHAPTER 4

Coltish Behavior

I WILL be glad when I no longer must smell each forkful of hay for mold before I feed it; when I can stop thinking about whether it is too cold or too windy to turn him out; and when I am no longer depressed by the sight of a not-empty feed pail. Yes, we have had trouble here. For about a month Jeffy has been having mild but recurrent bouts of diarrhea. This is very, very trying! It means road work has stopped and only milder forms of training can go on. Of course the Doc has been here. This is a big event because he has bred, raised, trained, shown, and judged horses and still does. I am glad of an excuse to get him, in his too busy life, and always have a long list of all kinds of questions to ask and thus pump him for his wisdom.

Jeffy is not seriously sick. He is just more quiet in his play and fussier in his eating. This last may result in part from all the mean tricks I have played with his food. He likes crimped oats with lots of molasses feed mixed with it, but this is what he should not have. So I have tried him on rolled oats. He thinks they are quite inedible. Crimped oats fed straight are similarly boring. The addition of a mixture of Vitamin B12 and other things makes the whole meal quite intolerable. We have reached a compromise on what is good for him and what is good to eat, and he is cleaning up his pail better. Fortunately, he takes his medicine very nicely squirted out of a rubber ear syringe into the corner of his mouth. The vitamin-plus mixture goes in that way too. He is now much better.

A new box stall is being built and the former manure pit converted into a shelter. In some lag in Jeffy's life I shall describe our expanded stable, which I think will be perfect now. We have even licked the wind problem I mentioned in the last chapter. From bitter experience, I suggest that if any of you are thinking of building a one-horse stable, which is what we did four years ago, at least plan, or better yet build, for expansion. It is much cheaper the first time. Here we are today ripping out a good, solid concrete floor, and messing up Toby's garage and carpentry area with garden tools, and making other expensive and inconvenient changes that might have been better foreseen. We would not be in this fix if I hadn't chosen for my one saddle horse a nice young versatile Morgan mare. If you have trouble getting across the idea of an apparently larger than necessary stable, you can say with perfect truth that a day and a night box stall and a pasture shelter for one horse are great conveniences. Don't forget space for the sleigh, buggy, and trailer in your planning, even if you think you will never drive and never cart your horse anywhere. If you get a Morgan, you will more than likely be doing both.

Before Jeffy's insides kicked up, I had taken him out on the road at night to get him used to night traffic. The shifting shadows thrown by the headlights bothered him more than the lights themselves. In about three trips he adjusted to them. It would have been easier with Bonnie, but I feel I have him in control better when I am on foot than when I lead him from her back. I am surprised how very rapidly he becomes accustomed to all sorts of new situations.

Within the last two weeks, I conditioned Bonnie for pleasure use after her six-month holiday. I take her out almost daily for an hour or so. She is full of pep and seems to enjoy this rest from maternity. This also serves to make Jeffy used to solitude. If I don't ride, I take him in and leave her out for a while. To say that they neighed for each other at first is a gross understatement; they screamed and made a frightful to-do—at least the one left at home did. Now Jeffy just calls when we leave and when he hears us return. With only the one stall, I have to be very careful that Bonnie is not at all heated when he nurses. As soon as this new stall is done, it will be easier. She can cool out there first.

Jeffy has had other useful training. His feet are handled often and he has had them rasped four times. He had his first ride by himself in the trailer. During his early leading practice he was led in and out of the trailer a great many times. He went to a show with his mother in August. This time, however, he was alone. Toby drove, and I rode with Jeffy. He was pretty frightened the first mile but soon calmed down.

He learned to step over at a pressure on the flank and the words "move over." This is very useful in stable handling, and it is the start of the pivot on the forehand and other movements that the heels, used separately, will require in later saddle training. The untrained horse instinctively moves against, not away from, pressure on the flank; and so this bit of training is a little harder than it would appear. It has automatically eliminated a bad stable habit that had started—crowding. Like his mother, Jeffy wants no interference while he eats his grain. Since eating in peace is important to good digestion, I never groom or bother them more than necessary. But I have to be able to work around them, and here was this tiny little bit of spunk laying his ears back and trying to get me against the wall. I hate to make an issue of a problem, especially in the stable, if it can be avoided. The "move over" signal absolutely dissolved that problem.

Now we have another behavior problem that I probably can eliminate quietly and peacefully in the same way. Jeffy, as I have said, ceased to kick after the first week or two of his life. I have seen his small heels fly right up in his mother's face when she bit him in the buttock for some infringement of her nursing rules. Now he kicks at neither of us, but when he is cross, he turns and runs his fat little behind into us. This is a very funny performance he very often does to Bonnie, who pays no attention, except for the move over. I am sure the potential problem will just evaporate like crowding did. I suspect a good deal of serious crowding may have started merely because the horse has not learned, against his instinct, to move away and not toward pressure on his side.

15

This should be taught quietly and patiently in regular lessons and not in a burst of panic as he leans and presses against you.

His spontaneous activities are of two kinds, play and business. His play ranges from a toss and a shake of his head and shoulders to a pell-mell tear around the pasture, varied with neat flying changes of lead, rears, bucks, and plunges, all with frills on them. He tries to get his mother playing too, much to her annoyance, by biting and bumping her. His business activities are practice in stallion skills. He has been mounting her since he was a few weeks old. This she accepts with more patience than his play. The other skill is what I call "herding." The wild stallion is said to drive and herd his mares, and I think I see Jeffy trying that when he bites Bonnie in the hocks and then flies at her head to turn her. There is something more serious in the way he goes at this than in his other play. Both she and he would benefit from the presence of other colts for him to play with and work on.

CHAPTER 5

Weaning, Winter Care,
Punishment

I HAVE been asked, "How big is Jeffy?" Today I borrowed a friend's measuring stick, and it shows that he is twelve hands, three inches at seven months and five days old. I have never measured him until today because there are so many things at home to measure him against. There was the first day that he reached the bottom of his mother's manger by sticking his tongue out. That manger is now his regular eating place. The five-foot stall partition was a gauge. It hid him for a long time. One day his soft upper lip showed over it, later his ears, and still later his eyes. He now throws his head over and hangs it there. All along I had a good idea how big he was, but it serves the record to know the hands and inches now and then.

Jeffy is weaned. It was a very simple and apparently painless process. At least we and the neighbors could sleep through it, and apparently the horses did too. It took six days by the gradual method. The first three nights he and Bonnie were together. In the daytime they were separated, except for nursing periods, at increasingly long intervals—four, six, and eight hours. Then they were also separated at night and the intervals between nursing made longer. On Christmas Eve they were completely separate and Bonnie was drying up. He was weaned at a little over six months old. By this gradual method of weaning I did not have to milk out Bonnie, and both horses were peaceful as long as they could see or hear each other in the barn.

It is wonderful to have Bonnie back as a pleasure horse. I ride nearly every day and have had two wonderful sleigh rides. The number of people who stop riding in winter surprises me. I have always ridden as much in winter as in summer. I remember as a child the torture of cold fingers and toes. Now I encase them in sheepskin and use a rubber pad to cover the metal of the stirrup. Several layers of thin, loose clothing for the whole body as well as two or three pairs of thin gloves, also loose, works well too.

I shoe Bonnie with pin caulks, which I change myself when they become blunt. I like to use leather pads in front because the snowballs are thrown out more quickly. Sometimes I grease or oil the pads if the snow is the type that balls badly. Caulks might be dangerous for horses turned out loose together. I have never had two horses to turn out together up to now. The danger of a horse caulking itself depends, I think, on the horse. Bonnie takes good care of herself; she is serene and fairly light and well balanced. Even so, she did caulk herself very slightly once. That was my fault because I was trying to longe her clockwise, and she cuts up then. They both do. I think it is because you have to stand on their off side and it confuses and upsets them, whereas counterclockwise is all right.

I am not trying to tell anyone what to do; I am merely saying what I do and what I think. I am not, therefore, suggesting you shoe with pin caulks. I have a friend who swears by drive caulks, which are blades instead of points. Later I used Mordex caulks, which I find best of all. Horse owners all have theories they will defend to the death.

Now I am surely going to offend some of your theories about the education of a colt. I have struck little Jeffy with a crop, yes and hard. He became a little demon at about six and a half months old, biting and rearing in a most alarming way. All was going fine; then one day he reared and struck me on the head. I put that down to longeing clockwise and paid no attention. Next day out on the road, he bit and reared at least six times within a couple of blocks. The following day I led him in the pasture, and he was so frightful that I got him back just as quick as I could and still save face. I was just plain scared. "This is a pretty pass," I said to myself, "if I can't handle him at six months old. If he is not corrected now someone else is going to give him a very rough time later."

The next day I went into the stall with a nice, wide crop and I led him around. When he bit or reared, I smacked once, hard, on the neck or shoulder. This happened four or five times within the ten minutes we walked. Next day we did the same thing, and I had to correct him a couple of times. We went round and round and in figure eights. Then I took him outdoors and had to punish him again for the first couple of days. Now he is well behaved; but I have only had him on the road once because the ice and snow interferes with the security of my own footwork, let alone his. I was interested to see that he never resented this punishment. However, I made sure before I struck him that he knew he had done wrong and that the punishment followed immediately. I never hit him more than twice, usually just once, so that he would not forget the cause in a panic. Right or wrong the system worked; we are back in a pleasant relationship. I am not afraid of him and he is not afraid of me. He lets me catch him anytime I want to in the pasture. In fact, he usually walks up to join me.

I have mentioned longeing Jeffy. I do not want to leave the impression that he is longeing correctly and at speed. He is too young for that. I am told that it is hard on young hocks. We have merely started circling slowly at a walk. That will be another chapter.

CHAPTER 6

~w~w~w~w~w~w~w~w~w~w~w~w~w~w~w~w~w~w~w~w~w~w~w~w~w~

Cast in the Stall,
Use of the Nose Chain

BOTH my horses recently have been cast in their stalls. This is a familiar predicament to experienced horsemen. To the new horse owner the sight of his friend lying helpless against a wall is an appalling spectacle, especially with the knowledge that without aid the horse cannot arise and that in this position the viscera may be so abnormally displaced as to cause death.

Both Bonnie and Jeffy are quiet horses in the stable. I was, therefore, much surprised early one morning to hear a pounding noise. I rushed to the barn and found poor little Jeffy wedged into a corner of his stall with his hind legs waving in the air and his forelegs thrashing against the wall. He stilled as I entered. I flung my arms around his neck and pulled him about a foot away from the wall. This was enough so that he could get a purchase on the floor. He jumped up and nipped me, clear evidence that all was well.

A few nights ago, Toby and I returned unexpectedly early from an evening engagement. All was quiet in the stable adjoining the garage; but as it was close to the time of my evening visitation, I went there to check up on the horses. Jeffy was up and seemed a little restless. I stood up on tiptoe to look over into Bonnie's stall. My heart leapt with fear. She was lying absolutely still, parallel to one wall, partly on her back and partly on her off side. "Toby," I called, "Bonnie's cast." By reaching over her, we worked the webbing longe line down below her off legs, which were crumpled against the wall. She made no move at all; she was completely limp, but she was warm and breathing. Together we put our weight and our strength on the webbing and pulled her right over. With her feet thus freed from the wall, she was able to get up and did so at once.

A horse usually becomes cast in a stall because he tries to roll all the way over and, in doing so, lands too close to the wall either to roll back or to get his feet under him to get up. A horse is more likely, they say, to be cast in a new stall because he has not had time to "take its measure." You read and hear of various ways to help a cast horse. For example, a block and tackle can be used to move the horse, by the tail if necessary. A wrecking tool can break out partitions. In big stalls straw can be heaped along the walls and in the corners to make a bowl-shaped bed, out of which it is hard for a horse to roll. Some stables are made with removable partitions in slots. A livery stable formerly in this town kept on hand a long board padded with a blanket. The board was used to press the legs of a horse cast in a straight stall down onto the floor, so that his thrashing would wriggle him into a position to rise. All these suggestions come from more experienced heads than mine, so I pass them on to you.

Now, however, I cannot withstand myself from also passing on a discovery of my own. Does your horse snatch at his tie ropes? Does your colt carry his lead line in his mouth or grab at it every few minutes? All you need to do is rub the rope or the leather or the chain with yellow, naphtha bar soap. Renew it every other day for a few days, and I think you will find these habits dropped. This soap was used to discourage mice and their chewing in my childhood home, so I tried it. It works with both Bonnie and Jeffy and is so much nicer to use than other recommended substances. I much prefer it to the punitive nagging, which this mild misdemeanor tends to induce.

Speaking of misdemeanors leads me back to Jeffy. You may remember that since he was a few weeks old he has been led with no trouble whatsoever both from foot and

21

from horseback, in fields and in traffic, day and night. Then at six and a half months he asserted his independence by rearing and biting. I reported on our showdown on this. As a result he appears to have no inclination to rear at all or to deliver one of those slashing bites. He still nips, but that is another matter. However, at eight months the age of revolt was not yet over. He discovered that if he suddenly bolted out and then swung in a half circle with the pull of the lead, he could create a fine mess of a situation, especially if he did this over and over again. The effect can only be appreciated with experience, but the result is that you get practically nowhere on your route, and that with great effort. It was high time for the best-known cure-all for leading troubles, that is, the chain of the lead strap over the nose. With this, either his run out or my jerk bangs the chain against the bone of his nose. He learned almost at once, and now he leads as light as a feather in my hand.

I wouldn't want you to think that Jeffy is mean. He is not at all mean, but at present he is in a stage of rebellion against control. He is trying to assert his rights, which he interprets as complete liberty. At the moment, however, we are in a state of love and charity with each other. What will happen next month remains to be seen.

CHAPTER 7

ᴐᴎᴐᴎᴐᴎᴐᴎᴐᴎᴐᴎᴐᴎᴐᴎᴐᴎᴐᴎᴐᴎᴐᴎᴐᴎᴐᴎᴐᴎᴐᴎᴐᴎᴐᴎᴐ

Parasites, Dogs,
and Other Education

ORMS. That is the subject today; not just any worms, nor even worms in other peoples' horses, but strongyles in Bonnie and Jeffy. One week ago I learned that my horses had worms. Why was I such an idiot as to think that my horses had no worms? Because a fecal sample from Bonnie tested two years ago was negative and fecal samples from both Bonnie and Jeffy analyzed this past fall were negative. (Negative, I presume, means that the level is below that needing treatment.) The report was not, I thought, surprising since no horses were pastured on this land for a great many years, until I brought Bonnie here about four years ago.

About a month ago I took a good look at Bonnie. She has always been an easy keeper, fat and sleek on very little grain. Now I found her a little thin, but she was getting more grain than she had ever had before her pregnancy. As for Jeffy, I didn't need to look at him. Something was wrong. Not only was he peaked but he was an off-again-on-again eater. His regular doctor was in the hospital. I talked to some friends with Morgans, and a group stopped in while they were in this area. Jeffy looked wormy was the verdict. I collected another sample from both horses and took them around to a new doctor. Then I sat at home for four days biting my nails while he coped with everyone else's emergency. He came at last. Yes, Jeffy was loaded with strongyles. Poor little Jeffy. This was the probable cause of all his troubles of which I told you. So now at the end of March they are both on phenothiazine. By May I hope very much Jeffy will again be a fat, bouncy colt. I feel badly that Jeffy had to be the guinea pig for me to learn on. What a lot there is to this business of horses!

We leave tomorrow for a trip to Arizona where I shall ride western every day for nearly the first time in my life. I ride a flat saddle because I learned in England and later had a teacher from the Vienna Horse School. I also ride a flat saddle because I live in the East where practically no one rounds up cattle or ropes calves, certainly not me, and where, therefore, the flat saddle is as natural as the western saddle is elsewhere. I like to see an experienced and able western horseman riding, but, alas, in these parts you see some pretty odd sights and bad horsemanship in a stock saddle. These same riders might have to ride a whole lot better in a flat saddle to survive on top, and that would be all to the good.

While we are gone, Bill has Bonnie and Jeffy. Although Billy is only in junior high, he is good for this job because he is dependable, he uses his head, he is quiet and gentle, and he is not afraid of them. When he started helping me about three years ago, he had had little experience with horses. I rather like that because he does things my way, knowing no other. I try to show him a little more than he will probably need.

In the course of Jeffy's nine months of life he has had experiences of which I have not yet spoken. He has become accustomed to the sound of cap pistols. Children came and fired so many that he now just stands at the pasture rail being petted while they shoot them off right there. He knows all about flying newspapers. On two windy days I released sheet after sheet—at first far from him, then close— finally leaving them to roll and waft about in the pasture while he played with them. I think I may have made a mistake on dogs, though. On three days I engaged a very small boy to come bringing his very large collie. Until we finally restrained him with a leash, the collie would rush at Jeffy, roaring; Jeffy would flee for a few jumps and then turn and rush at the collie. Even after three days no peaceful settlement seemed near, so the business was called off. At least Jeffy will never meet any louder dogs.

These things might be risky with a more nervous colt. I have done them because Jeffy is not at all inclined to panic. He is a bold little horse. Furthermore, our fences are plainly visible. I have heard of colts so terrified that they have dashed themselves into fences and been very seriously injured. Also all introductions have been gradual—even the dog, though Jeffy has met others in his walks with me on the road.

We have one problem that may be more acute when only one colt is kept. Jeffy is a regular little dead-end kid in his play with me in the pasture. If I go out there when he is loose, at once he is bouncing up all around me and practically on top of me. He just wants something alive to play with, but he plays very rough. I suppose when there are more colts they work this off on each other. In businesslike handlings he is perfectly all right, but I discourage any unnecessary entrance into the pasture. When I go I take a lead line and snap it on if he gets too much for me. From others' remarks, I gather lots of single colts are like this.

CHAPTER 8

~~~~~~

The Horse Show

THIS is the show season. We are getting ready for The Show, the National Morgan Horse Show. Bonnie and Jeffy have already performed most satisfactorily in smaller shows. We brought no blues home but did collect a mess of assorted colors from six classes. So today I will talk about the work and rewards in this business of showing. However, before doing that, there are a few things I want to try to say. In the first place, I would not want any of you to think that I think I have a show horse in Bonnie. Neither nature nor I intend that we excel in the show ring. As a small-time adult amateur exhibitor, I am usually licked by the big exhibitors, breeders, and professionals. Do I resent this? Absolutely not. They have the horses and they spent the time, money, and have the experience necessary to get the blues and reds over and over again. They should and do win, almost always, over us casual hobbyists. The only question is who beats whom among them. I enjoy their struggles from inside the ring, as well as from outside. One more thought, and I will get down to business. To me a Morgan who is tops in the show ring is no less a Morgan than the one that herds cattle, plows, travels the trail, or teaches the children to ride. You might as well consider that the prize baby beef Hereford is less a Hereford than the one fattening in the pasture. Is the best-of-breed German shepherd any less a German shepherd than the one leading the blind or guarding the home? To me it is simply a matter of conformation, fitting, training, and what the owner wishes to make of his animal—but, un-

26

fortunately, competition often brings out the worst in breeders, owners, and handlers in artificializing the horse.

Showing a horse is an awful lot of work. I would not show unless my horse was in as good shape as I could get him. To me that means that he shines with health and my elbow grease, that his bones are well covered with fat and muscle, and that he has a good idea of what to do in the ring. All that means plenty of good food and hard work in grooming, conditioning, and training. Fortunately, the treatment with phenothiazine was completely effective so that now, in June, Bonnie and Jeffy are in fine shape. Jeffy has even picked up almost all the weight he should have. So we entered the season with the fundamentals of health.

Both horses are getting more grain. Jeffy, in any case, gets all he can clean up in three feedings. To muscle them they are exercised more. Jeffy is led out on the road with Bonnie two or three times a week. Bonnie goes out daily for either a good long trail ride, a shorter training ride, a few leaps over some low jumps, or a trip with Jeffy. The point of this conditioning and training is for in-hand and pleasure classes only. If I were doing saddle classes it would mean hours in a training ring. I am terribly handicapped this year, without a ring, even for pleasure classes. Working right close to the rail, which is so important in showing, can best be taught in a ring, as can the steady maintenance of the trot and canter around and around, on and on.

Bonnie is an old hand at showing. She is flawless in canter leads and in poising. The problem is getting her up in the bit and showing a little enthusiasm. Her attitude seems to be one of good-natured resignation in the show ring. Jeffy, of course, needs to know only how to lead in-hand, at which he is quite good, and to stand correctly, at which he is less good, being of a very enthusiastic and impetuous nature, as well demonstrated in the last show.

Grooming at this season is more regular. In fact, they are often groomed twice a day. After exercise a very thorough job is done because the dirt has been loosened and I get more out at that time. Grooming is only partly done for cleanliness; it also stimulates the blood vessels under the skin. Anyone who keeps a horse knows what a terrible job it is to clean up a neglected coat. It is much easier to keep it clean all the time. I wish I did that with tack, too.

A few days before the show, I trim the long hairs on the legs and remove the whiskers around the mouth. In this trimming I do not go as far as others because my horses still are pastured at least for part of the day or night. Therefore, I do not trim the long, protective hairs over the eyes nor trim out the inside of the ear. A day or two before the show I wash the horses. The day before the show is really a tough one, because it takes hours to clean dirty tack, especially harness. Then, too, the horses get their final grooming because experience has taught me that there is never time on the show day for more than a lick and a promise. That night I try to have everything packed and the trailer hitched up, all set to go.

Here is Bonnie standing in a proper stretched position.

Bonnie and I are practicing at the trot (above) and cantering at the correct lead (below).

Why do I show at all? What possible rewards are there for the effort and expense, especially since I do not aim for prize money or the top ribbons? (Don't misunderstand me. I like a blue as well as the next person, but I am not pained and surprised if I don't get it.) The first reward is the knowledge of and close relation with my horses. I enjoy the evening when I sit on the stable floor, all mixed up with their legs, trimming away. They seem to enjoy it, too. I think I have learned to judge condition better. The best way to learn to groom a horse thoroughly and quickly is to have to do it for a show. The rewards as far as Jeffy is concerned are obvious—his education and sophistication now at this early age of one year. Because of a few shows each year, Bonnie is a far better pleasure horse for me to ride around here casually. Why? Because I have had to teach her the elements of collection, of ready response, of obedience to leg and hand for the shows she was entered in. To be sure, I could do that without showing; but I am lazy and I have other interests, and to train solely for the goal of a well-trained horse is not immediate enough to make me get at it and stick with

Bonnie looks good at the National Morgan Horse Show.

Bonnie's a winner!

it. The last reward is the pleasure of experiencing all a Morgan has to offer. I bought a Morgan, knowing nothing of the breed, because I wanted one horse that, with minimum effort and expense, could give me the widest possible experience in the pleasure use of horses. I have ridden and driven Bonnie long and short distances, alone and in company; I have shown her; she has given me a colt; and now she is learning to jump. What more can anyone ask of any single horse than my Morgan mare has given to me?

CHAPTER 9

Jumping

BONNIE and I jumped for the first time in a show ring three days ago. With a score of two faults, we placed second. She jumped in quiet, graceful arcs with minimum effort. This is the hunter way of going rather than the open-jumper way. A hunter should jump smoothly, just skimming the jumps, because he may have to keep it up for a long time and should not wear himself or his rider out by needless effort. It takes years to make a good hunter. We do not have any such lofty ambitions, but I try to practice their sound principles in a very small way.

One summer when we were living in England, my mother rented a mousy little mare for me from the local livery stable. Neither Molly nor I had ever jumped, but we worked at it all summer because the first cub hunt of the season would be held a few days before I had to leave. I rigged up crude jumps in the pasture. Over these I first longed her and then rode her. Water jumps were the worst problem. I remember one long, tedious afternoon spent on the near side of a brook, from which location I was finally released by some gypsies who beat Molly over the stream. The hunt itself was a wonderful experience. Under the stimulus of hound and horn, Molly leapt like a deer. The jump I remember the best was my downfall. We came down a wooded lane at a fine canter to find it closed off by a hedge and bar. Molly sailed over the timber and plummeted down into a field two feet lower than the lane. I kept right on down her shoulder.

Jeffy watches with interest as Bonnie is schooled over the jumps.

More than twenty years have passed since then in which, although I have ridden, I have done no jumping. Prior to the time I bought her as a three-year-old and until she was bred the next year, Bonnie had a little schooling for a few months. This was interrupted by Jeffy and not resumed until this spring. The way that I have trained her may seem ridiculously gradual, but in principle it is the way hunters are trained.

A hunter has three goals. He must be quiet; he must be bold in the face of varied jumps; he must respect the danger in a jump. To ensure quietness, no jump was raised until Bonnie was thoroughly accustomed to a given height; for boldness, jumps were frequently varied in appearance, covering them with branches, blankets, etc.; for respect, all jumps were as nearly solid as could conveniently be made.

I started by laying a number of long poles on the ground. Over these Bonnie was led, walked free, or ridden until she ceased to touch them. The poles were then raised a few inches. A bar of her drop-bar gate between paddock and pasture was left on the ground, and she crossed it at walk, trot, and canter in her normal movements from the barn to pasture. It was then raised to the lowest slot. After a week or two, the second one was put in place making her really hop it as she came and went. Since it was solidly fixed she learned soon to respect it to avoid a sharp crack on her leg. On each side of the bar was a natural reward, food and water at one end, pasturage at the other. The bar itself provided punishment for careless jumping. Therefore, she learned that a small jump was a natural and easy way to get from one place to another, not a matter for excitement.

After a few weeks of this, I rigged up jumps as solid as possible in the pasture and led her, then longed her, and lastly rode her over them. Often the jumps were changed in appearance or location. They were still two feet or less. She never refused, but she did run out. When she ran out I quietly brought her back until she did go over. At this stage the important things to me were that she jump quietly and that she find no cause to get excited or to find the business distasteful. For the last reason all lessons were very short. I was as inexperienced at jumping as Bonnie. My problem was to be absolutely sure that no matter how awkwardly she jumped, I would not clutch at the reins and hurt her mouth, thus surely teaching her to refuse. To prevent this, I quite frankly hung on to her mane as she went over.

I decided I would like to try a jumping class at a show and, therefore, I should do something about my form. After a refresher course, Bonnie was up to about two feet, and she was doing nicely and ready to go higher. I had wished for some time to get instruction in the correct hunting seat from a competent teacher. In my early youth, I had excellent teachers of riding—two Englishmen and an Austrian. For anyone taking up riding, I believe that lessons from a really good teacher are the best possible investment; even a few lessons are better than none. Fortunately, we are within a few miles of an excellent instructor in jumping form. I could only work in four lessons before he went north, but they were a tremendous help. He assigned Fan-Tan to me. Fan-Tan is a little black mare who goes straight and true at jumps with never a thought of refusing or running out. With boldness and vigor she hurled me over and fielded me neatly on the far side. Every once in a while I had a hint of the wonderful feeling it would be to be "with my horse" all the way.

As she jumps, Bonnie demonstrates her versatility and style.

When he returns I shall take more lessons, because I have gotten into bad habits since he left.

While my lessons were going on, I jumped Bonnie free in the paddock. After a brief warm-up on the longe I let her loose and, swishing a whip, sent her over two jumps in sequence in the ninety- by fifty-foot area. Two laps one way, reverse, and two laps the other way, if done well, constituted a lesson. The jumps were varied in appearance from

35

time to time. They were made quite solidly of stacked-up cinder blocks with poles wedged in the holes. She knew it if she hit them. Bonnie gave every indication of enjoying this activity.

When my lessons ended I started to ride Bonnie over the jumps. I made a temporary ring using fabric tape for the rail. Around the rail I put four of the cinder block jumps and added two smaller ones in the middle. She was jumping three feet free by this time. For the first few rides, I lowered the jumps so she could adjust her balance to my weight at a lower height. A week before the show I did my first double round—eight jumps at three feet or a little higher. Again I was careful not to excite, bore, or tire her in the lessons. We never did more than sixteen of the rail jumps, with possibly four of the little jumps, with a rest between each double round.

I now decided that Bonnie knew her job; no longer could she run out without unpleasant consequences. She must learn that she could take the jump on the first try. Below three feet she had seldom run out and only from an upset to her conservatism. At three feet she started to run out more, even with no change in appearance or position of the jump. On about five separate occasions I gave her one hard smack with my crop right behind the girth. For such a quiet mare this resulted in a volcanic explosion hard to control with a snaffle, but when the dust settled she just sailed over the disputed jump. At the show I felt her consider a run out at the first jump, but it was only revealed in a little awkwardness at that jump. Just before entering the ring I put her through a long serpentine of about a dozen loops at the walk as a refresher course of obedience to hand and leg, and that may also have helped.

In all this, Jeffy was an interested spectator.

Our hard work was worth the effort. Bonnie wins the jumping class at the National Morgan Horse Show.

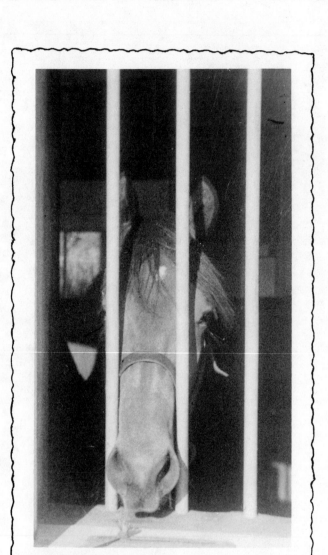

Jeffy is a yearling stallion, June 30, 1953.

CHAPTER 10

Growth in Body,
Mind, Spirit

JEFFY'S growth, like that of all young animals, is not just a continuous allover increase in size. Some parts grow faster at one time and then other parts at latter times. Because of this process, at thirteen months of age he has lost the proportions that make up the characteristics of a baby. His body has caught up with his legs, his neck with his head, and—by other less obvious changes—he now looks like a little horse instead of a foal. His expression has changed. The early look of innocence and fragility is being replaced by one of greater assurance and nobility.

His deportment, too, has changed. The coltish trick of rushing us and pestering us in the pasture is gone, as well as the amusing habit he had of rollicking about in his stall, rearing and squealing to attract my attention while I worked in the stable. During his most playful stages when he was left alone most of the time, I tried to see if he would amuse himself with a big red rubber ball. No, only if I threw it would he chase it, and even so the sport soon palled. He always has and still does play by the hour with fallen twiggy branches in his pasture. I used poplar because old-timers thought that poplar wood was a vermicide. During the first days of his weaning, I kept one in the stall, and the frequent sound of its slapping on the wooden walls assured me that he was not too unhappy. Apparently, a branch is a more satisfactory plaything than a ball because he can get his teeth in the wood and throw it around. He still puts everything in his mouth—ropes, chains, reins, trousers, shirts, and human skin. The naphtha soap had no lasting deterrent effect on this habit, although in Bonnie's case it has largely stopped her habit of running the cross-tie ropes through her teeth when I groom her. Jeffy's youth is still revealed in his high-pitched voice calling us when we leave him. When I disturb them by entering the stable while they sleep, he complains in a little soprano whine, whereas Bonnie groans deeply.

Now at a little over one year of age, his attentions to Bonnie are hardly more marked than before he was first separated from her. They have been separated since December, but our aisles are narrow and he can easily touch her as I lead her out or groom her. Under these circumstances he does a moderate amount of ranting around with soft and passionate conversation. It is no problem, merely giving spice to our stable life. I may, however, have to give up leading him while I ride Bonnie until he is better trained.

I entered Jeffy in a second show this year. This show was thirty miles away, the longest distance he has ever traveled by trailer. He is an excellent traveler, and he has taught Bonnie how to get into a trailer without making a scene. For this show I did not rent a stall, wishing him to learn the tedium of hours in the trailer relieved by a little walking around and grazing. The conditions were frightful—at first hot enough to cause sweat to pour off the horses, later a fierce wind, thunderstorm, and driving rain. He was perfectly all right the next day but very sleepy.

His learning is like that of other growing animals—an advance, a smaller retreat, and then a bigger advance. Every now and then his wild little spirit seems to call out, "No, no, I won't," but he does and we are at peace. He has for some months been used to a padded surcingle lightly girthed about him, which I have put on for short periods once in a while. About the same time I put on the surcingle, when he must have been about ten months, I put a small jointed snaffle in his mouth and left it there for a half hour or so while he was loose in his stall. I repeated that about ten times for longer periods up to an hour and a half. The first few times he worked and worked to spit it out, and his tongue was over the bit more often than under. To stop that I put grain in his manger so he would have to get his tongue down and under to eat. I had no trouble at all putting on the bit; I know I did not need the salt that I had rubbed on my hand and on the bit, but possibly it made this first introduction pleasanter to him.

About a month ago, I started longeing him. The problem of starting him in the clockwise direction was easily solved by leading him from the off side enough to accustom him to my presence there. The other problem was to keep him away from me and at an even distance so I would not have to make constant adjustments on the rein. A flick of the whip on his shoulder taught him to stay out. Yes, I do use a long-lashed whip but I do not beat him. It is an aid to keep him out and to keep him moving briskly, now that he knows his job, and to see that he does not get into a habit of just slopping along any old way. Do not imagine that he moves at all three gaits at a word of command or reverses on command. No, indeed, he does not. We even have scenes in which he decides that he wants to go the other way or just run out. I would never dare do this with a rope either for my hands or his hide. No, a nice wide webbing gives me the courage to brace myself and hang on. With just the halter to hold him, he can really take off and take me with him.

The next stage was to longe him with the bit and bridle on over the halter but the rein still on the halter. I do not want to hurt his mouth. At present we have advanced another step. I run two side reins from the surcingle to his bit. These side reins are so loose that all they hinder is his reach to the ground or sidewise to bite the reins. Only when he has progressed to the use of a checkrein, a long time from now, will I tighten the side reins. Otherwise, he will flex his neck at the crest, much too low. Meanwhile, his mouth is getting some experience with the pull of the bit and a little toughening of the soft young tissues.

The last step has been to drive him very slowly at the walk in long reins. In three lessons he has begun to get the idea of the turns. All these things he learned in a very gradual way, with just the shortest of lessons, sometimes only ten minutes. I try to follow the good advice never to start anything new unless the colt is entirely calm and relaxed. I probably stop before I have to in order to avoid, if possible, a flare-up and an issue that would then have to be battled out. So far I have had no second person to assist. At present he is really a very good little colt and I am pleased with him.

CHAPTER 11

Coltish Behavior and
Long-Rein Driving

JEFFY is now fourteen months old. At half this age, seven months ago, he measured twelve hands, three inches; today he stands fourteen hands, one inch. Except for his tendency to nip, he is a very well behaved little colt. He is fearless, not easily upset, and quick to learn. I am told that in one way I am fortunate to have a stallion to train because I do not have the problem of timidity so frequent in fillies. He certainly does appear to be afraid of nothing. I can lead him or drive him right by a baler at work or through a footpath in a strange wood, and he merely watches these new sights with eager attention. On the other hand, a verbal reproof means nothing to him; and he often dares me to challenge him, although less often than earlier. He seems to enjoy getting a rise out of me. Any attention is better than none, short of a really sharp smack. That is why the nipping is so hard to cure.

On the other hand, in all businesslike handlings he is very well behaved. Today, for example, I spent nearly a half hour getting bot eggs off his legs by safety razor and fingernail. He was perfectly quiet as I squatted on my haunches by each of his legs. Not once, so far, has he ever raised a single forefoot to strike as do so many stallions. At six months of age, he reared up and struck with both forefeet at me, and on extreme provocation I have seen him strike at a dog with both forefeet. That was what I call his age of revolt, and I

had to take strong disciplinary measures with him. His dis-
inclination to use his forefeet is seen also in the fact that he
seldom paws. His stall bears no signs of excavation. In a
strange stall at his first show this year he wanted to get out
terribly; but instead of digging, as many horses do, he threw
himself bodily at the door. By this very effective method he
burst off five of the little wooden crosspieces used to fasten
it. We had to wedge a section of telegraph pole against the
door. Thus firmly confined, he very quickly quieted down
and merely watched with alert interest during the rest of
the show.

I had intended to have him gelded this fall, but he is so
easy to handle and so little of a problem that I will probably
let him develop longer. I cannot, however, turn him and
Bonnie out simultaneously in adjacent lots separated only by
a railing without watching them constantly. That is a great
nuisance in our daily life. Prior to the show he was out, with
access to his stall, all night and a short while in the day. Now
he is out both day and night, except for a few hours when
Bonnie has her turn at the grass.

After about ten short lessons in long reins he drives quite
nicely. He graduated from paddock to pasture to our open
land and lastly to the road as he learned to turn in response
to the reins and as the need for long straightaways for free
walking became manifest. At first, hesitant with ignorance
about this business of driving, he wove from right to left and
dragged one foot after the other. The turns were quickly
learned; "Whoa" and "steady" are old familiar terms to
which he has long responded promptly. The fast, free, flat-
footed walk straight ahead was the real problem. I used long
straightaways with nothing to impede forward movement.
Now, except in strange territory, he moves out quite well.
For this reason I have not yet used a checkrein or bitting
harness. All I want now is prompt forward movement. Action and head carriage will have to come later.

He is, however, naturally a good deal more of a peacock
than Bonnie. After walking a while as I drive him, I then
practice him at the trot as he moves around me, both ways.
So far I have discouraged cantering either in long reins or on
the longe. I am pleasantly surprised by how little he acts up

in these short elementary training lessons. He may jog a bit and toss his head or on the longe buck a little; but with "steady" it soon passes. I am sure I could hitch him to a vehicle anytime; but as you know by now, I take it very slow and easy. Furthermore, I feel he is too young to take any weight yet.

May I say once again that I am not presuming to tell you how to break a colt. I tell only what I happen to do with my particular individual and the theories I have. This is merely the journal of my daily life with my first colt and his dam, Bonnie. There are many good books on training. I own a few and will mention them as they have been a great help to me. *Practical Horse Breeding and Training* by Jack Widmer has been useful since before Jeffy was born. It deals with thoroughbreds for hunting and polo, but the early chapters are appropriate for any breed and include early driving lessons. The classic work for saddle-type horses for show is by Earl Farshler and is called *Riding and Training*. This is the second volume in a two-volume set; the first is *History of the American Saddlebred Horse*. The U.S. Cavalry manual issued from Fort Riley, Kansas entitled *Horsemanship and Horsemastership* sets a very high standard of riding and training and is a very useful book.

For schooling for jumping, both the first and third above are helpful. My favorite, however, is the well-known British work *Training Hunters, Jumpers and Hacks* by Harry D. Chamberlain. Excellent, too, is *Be a Better Horseman* by Captain Vladimir S. Littauer. This has the disadvantage of being entirely in dialogue, which makes it very hard to use for quick reference. Captain Littauer has other books, not so written, but I do not happen to own them. The sections on riding in his books are, of course, for forward-seat riders, but his sections on training for general handiness and jumping are very clear. The clearest directions for the hunting seat that I have read are in Gordon Wright's *Learning to Ride, Hunt and Show*. All these books have been published within the last ten years. Public libraries, especially in cities, sometimes have a fine collection of old horse books, many of which are excellent.

45

CHAPTER 12

Colic

JEFFY has just passed through the Valley of the Shadow of Death. Is that too strong an expression for an attack of colic? I think not. Colic has claimed the life of many colts, and horses too.

I had not properly diagnosed the signs of trouble the night before—an unusual crankiness and irritability, a touch of diarrhea. On that morning, not expecting trouble and being very busy, I hardly saw him. I gave him an enormous feed of grain for breakfast and turned him out. It was after lunch that his conduct first surprised me. He was lying down in his pasture, stretched out flat. Jeffy almost always takes his naps in his stall, since the door is usually open. I led him in for grooming and a little long-rein work. My second surprise came when he tagged along behind me quietly with never a nip. Cross-tied on the barn floor he drooped and his legs seemed to buckle under him. I put him in his stall and down he dropped and rolled. I fled to the phone. Fortunately the doctor was in and would come at once.

Back in the stable I found Jeffy cast. Little did I know that in the next twelve hours he would be cast again and again and again and that both of us would have less and less strength to uncast him as the hours went on. Sometimes I would pull him away from the wall by the halter, sometimes by the tail. It would take the doctor at least a half hour to come the twenty miles. I consulted with a knowledgeable friend as to what to do until then. We decided that I should lead Jeffy. Around and around we went in the shade of the hickory trees in the pasture. Every now and then Jeffy would nudge my hand to hint that we should stop so he could lie down. Each time he did go down it was harder to get him up.

How welcome was the sound of the doctor's car! Jeffy had a fever and he had a pain in his insides. He was first given a shot of an antibiotic, then he got a big capsule, then he got a whole flock of purple pills to fight the toxins that might be building up in his digestive tract. After each treatment he collapsed with a heavy thud, rolled, and almost always got cast. Unlike reports of other kinds of colic, I never saw him thrashing, nor did he kick or bite at his stomach, although he looked at it. Of course this more violent behavior may have been going on all morning when I did not see him. By the time he was under treatment he was a very, very sick and weary colt. The doctor stayed almost an hour watching him. Then he left and said he would come back later. I was not to mind if Jeffy lay down. If he rested quietly I should leave him down but not cast. If he started thrashing I was to try leading him a little. So all afternoon Jeffy was down most of the time. He got up only to try and find greater comfort in a new place to lie. I led him a little, but after a few steps he would be down. The doctor had gone to a new emergency about thirty miles away, so I had little hope of seeing him again soon. His wife called at five for a report. I said Jeffy was the same. At about six the doctor was back and gave Jeffy two quarts of mineral oil by stomach tube and then left. I was to report at eight-thirty.

After the second visit Jeffy was down even more. He seldom got up to readjust his position. I hoped this new behavior came under the category of resting quietly; anyway, I left him alone while I got supper and did the dishes. Now that Toby was home to help, Jeffy only got cast once. At eight-thirty I reported Jeffy still down. The doctor came again and gave another flock of purple pills. We had a terrible time to get him up for this. Miraculously, however, once up he stayed there, swaying, with drooping head and half-closed eyes. To give him an illusion of support, I hooked the lead strap to his halter and dropped it over the partition. Still he stood, he raised his head, he even pricked his ears at Bonnie across the aisle. This was the first time that he had been free of pain since I saw his condition at about noon, ten hours earlier. After warning me that Jeffy might have a relapse, but that his condition seemed definitely better, the doctor left. No sooner had he gone than the relapse came, and Jeffy was down again. An hour later, however, I found him standing quietly in his usual resting corner for a second time at peace with his insides. I gave him some water and led him on a clean shavings bed with not even a spear of straw to eat.

Next day he seemed all right but quiet. I think it took him a full week to recover entirely, and during that time I brought him back very gradually to nearly his full diet.

What caused this attack? I do not know. I had made no change in his diet prior to it. I found little knots of moldy clover in some of our hay bales, which might have been a cause. I had been graining him heavily and in only two feedings, so that in each feeding he got a great mass of food. It could have been that such a mass landing on a disordered digestive tract brought on the acute attack. Now I feed him in three feedings and a somewhat smaller total. I have never told how much I feed my horses, because I do not feel that I know enough to be a guide. Apparently the best guide is the condition of the horse, but that takes time to show. I suspect I was dropping too big a load on Jeffy's small stomach right along.

CHAPTER 13

∽∿∽∿∽∿∽∿∽∿∽∿∽∿∽∿∽∿∽∿∽∿∽∿∽∿∽∿∽∿∽∿∽∿∽∿∽

How Stupid Can I Be?
First Driving

"WHOA, Whoa, WHOA!" The sound of wood splitting and the crash of trampled bushes were incongruous noises in an otherwise peaceful and jet black night. What could have possessed me? I hitched up Jeffy for the first time on a night as black as ink, without any help, and to a jerry-built rig. To make matters worse, I didn't even use the pasture but went right out down the drive, or planned to. This is not the way to break a colt to drive.

I think this action of mine must have been a compensatory behavior—an extreme of foolishness to counterbalance the extreme of stable virtue displayed earlier in the day. That morning I read an article entitled something like this, "Don't Booby-Trap Your Horse." It was a good article. It pointed out all the little things in and around stables on which a horse could hurt himself. I had such booby traps and I set about eliminating them. First I replaced the old loosened rings on which the cross-tie ropes are fastened. Then I renewed the loose sill board in Jeffy's stall. I moved the bridle cleaning hook to a less prominent place. I did a number of other similar things. By supper time I was bloated with pride. After the dishes were done and Toby had gone up to his study, time hung heavy on my hands. I went back to the stable to see what more I could do. I cleaned and trimmed both horses. There was Jeffy cross-tied right in front of the carriage doors, all ready to go, and there was the travois I had built also all ready to go. Why not put them together? Hereafter, I count to a hundred before giving way to such inspirations.

I should explain about this travois. Like other one- or two-horse owners I do not have the variety of tack needed for the stages in the life of a young horse. Since this will probably be my only young horse, I do not wish to buy such things as a breaking cart, breaking harness, bitting harness, and those other large and rather expensive temporary items. So I borrow what I can and try to make do in other ways. A drag, something like an Indian travois, has been used by some of the best people, so to speak, in the Morgan world. The trouble was I had never gotten a good description of one until too late. About the only thing right with mine was the big, strong carriage bolts that I used to attach the spacer to the poles. The spacer, instead of being a pine board, should have been a good strong piece of plank, and the poles should have been longer and should have been well padded at the shoulder end.

Well, here stood Jeffy, nice and quiet. So I very carefully pulled up the drag on him. Still no trouble. I opened both doors wide and put on the lead strap over his nose. I was going to lead him instead of driving him at first. I unhooked him from the cross-ties and we took a few tentative steps forward. Now I should go back and explain that this was not really the first time he was asked to pull long objects. A few times, including that very morning, he pulled corn or sunflower stalks with the big leaves rustling and slapping at his legs. We had had no trouble in these daylight ventures in the paddock. I did notice that he was upset by the pressure of the ends on his shoulders when we turned, but I had always stopped him and straightened them out before going forward again. Anyway, they were light and the pressure didn't amount to much. I knew the poles would be another matter, but the spacer was supposed to keep the poles parallel to each other and to him on the turns. As I said, we sallied forth about five steps into the black of night. There was a rending noise. The spacer snagged on the sill and the pine split. The next five minutes seemed like eternity and were one horrible blur of turmoil. The only thing I could think of was "hang on" and I did. First we plunged through a shrubbery border, then through our precious hedge of *Juniperus chinensis columnaris* and then the vegetable garden. My nearly dead weight on his nose brought him plunging around the circumference of a circle, and so we went around and around through the bushes, the hedge, and the garden. At last he stopped, both of us were panting and shaken. With soothing words and calming hands, I unhitched him and put him away. Later I will report on how this matter progressed.

Meanwhile, Jeffy learned about wire. He knows that sometimes it bites. In order to be able to turn both horses out at the same time, I had to put up an electric fence to keep the little stallion away from the wooden fence that contains Bonnie. He treats this wire with great caution, which I hope he will extend to all wire he may encounter the rest of his life. Unfortunately, he also learned that it does not always bite. It is so arranged that when he has both paddock and pasture for his use the circuit is off because the gate is open. I will have to reroute the circuit so that even with an open gate the wire is charged around the rest of the enclosure.

In a few days both horses will be wormed. For twenty-four hours ahead of time they must be starved—no food of any kind. These will be long hours for me. I will hardly dare go into the stable. A good many months ago I treated them both for pinworms to see if I could check their tail rubbing. I think it did help, but they are back in Bonnie. I see them often under her tail. I will have to do it again. Jeffy is back on medicine for bloodworms. Apparently, if you have limited pasturage in constant use, you have worms in your horses. This journal is written for the likes of me, people with a horse or two, not a lot of land for their use, and not much experience. Personally, I think we have a few problems more than the breeder in raising and training, don't you?

CHAPTER 14

Judging a Horse Show

YESTERDAY Bonnie ran away in harness with her tail clamped firmly over the near line. Thanks to her basic serenity, no problem. The day before I festooned Jeffy with Bonnie's full harness, including the breeching, for the first time. A trial spin with long reins in the pasture was uneventful, so I drove him out on the road. All went well until a Morgan filly saw him from her adjacent pasture. What screams of joy and ardor from both horses! What a flapping and slapping of straps and buckles! What nimble footwork I needed! What a life for a middle-aged woman! I pass on to another subject.

On a Friday night Mr. George Nichols called me up and asked me to judge his school show on Sunday. All classes were horsemanship classes; all contestants, except in the family class, were children. He was in a bad spot. The invited judge was unable to come, and he could get no other on such short notice. I was in a bad spot too, since although I had never judged before I could not refuse him. I was far too much indebted to him for help with my horses. He invited me to bring whomever I wished to help. I declined. I would have been glad to understudy an experienced judge, but I foresaw the added problems of working with someone who knew no more than I.

I was not worried about the basic information, namely, the points of equitation, the movements to call for in the ring, and the requirements for age classes. What did worry me were what I will call technical problems of judging, and I was right to worry. Under this term I include methods of quick, clear notation on the card, how to weigh the relative value of faults and virtues, and lastly and worst how to identify the contestants at any point in the ring. Because of these problems I think a performance judge should have a period of apprenticeship by some system such as the AHSA (American Horse Show Association) now has. I think only practice can solve these problems to the point where a performance judge can cope with a big class. By a performance class I mean one in which contestants are in constant and simultaneous motion. This covers my equitation classes except that the riders, not the horses, are judged.

As a spectator, I had never visualized these technical problems. The judge is given a card both to record the placings and to note the performance of the entries. The problem of notation is the development of some system of clear symbols so that each entry has a record, which I suppose could be filed only in the judge's mind, from the moment the class starts. Otherwise, the danger is that the placings will be made on the last thing the judge observes before the lineup. In a performance class, you can't eliminate at the start because a bad walk may be offset by a good trot and so on. I should think that in a breed class you could eliminate on type and general conformation at first glance and thus cut the group down.

The second problem applies to all judging of anything, that is, the relative degree of faults and virtues. As far as I can see, there is only one way to solve this problem: make up your mind what you think is worse and what you think is better. Decide from personal bias or prejudice. What other possible way could there be to solve it? For example, to me "paciness" in a Morgan is bad, so if he tends to pace at a trot it's thumbs-down to me, even if he walks and canters like a dream. Paciness is inherited so I think that is not a bad prejudice for a Morgan horse. A judge I know favors strongly small ears and will place an attractive head over a good rear, and so it goes. We tend to have our ideal in our mind.

Equitation classes bring out other prejudices. In my show, two little girls go by. One holds her hands vertically like candle holders; the other appears to be holding a rolling pin, with her hands horizontally. Of course, the happy medium is better, but of the two faults I think the rolling pin is worse. It seems to me that the only possible solution to placing these faults is up to the individual prejudice of the judge, and why not? The exhibitor shows under more than one judge, and a show committee should try different judges, other things being equal, for each show. This problem is the one that makes a good case for more than one judge to a class.

The third problem is the one that really floored me. Sometimes, in the classes of more than six entries, it made me want to walk out of the ring and never come back again. It is the problem of identifying the contestants. I know that with experience a judge develops a system that becomes serviceable for nearly any size class. But imagine that you are a judge. You stand near the track, because that is the only place where you can see the numbers, and then only when the rider has passed you. Ten or so riders, all strangers, are going around at the gaits you call for. One comes toward you, alone. You get a good look. You turn to watch for her number. You look down and make a note of the performance on your card. You look up, a bunch of three are right in front of you. You have entirely missed what they were doing, so although you can see their numbers, you have no notation. Too late. You look across the ring and there is a child on the wrong canter lead. You can't keep all cantering until wrong-lead gets around so you can see her number. You call for a walk, thinking you can pick it up anyway as she goes by. Meanwhile, a couple get in the way, and you've lost her. Maybe that gives you some idea of what a new judge is up against. Of course, through the whole business you also have the pressure of time on your mind.

Actually, identification became a little easier as the show went on. Possibly it would have been better if I had not tried to impersonalize the riders into sets of hands, legs, and seats, if I had quite frankly looked at them as boys and girls with different faces and different clothing. I knew just one of the entries. Wherever she was, I could identify her. I'm afraid it didn't help her. She is a good rider, but three out of four times when I happened to look at her in the trot, she was on the wrong diagonal. She went down to third place. It is quite possible that first and second were also now and then on the wrong diagonal but were lost among the unidentified.

I saw the necessity of rating faults in the advanced jumping class. One girl jumped quite well and with confidence but her legs were in front of the girth, a bad fault. Another girl was obviously under sound and thorough schooling but, as is the way of teachers, the correctness of her seat had been exaggerated way beyond the size of the jump. She looked as if she was going to take five feet instead of two and a half. Furthermore, this was still such a new business to her that lots of daylight showed between crotch and saddle. I had to decide this, didn't I, by personal bias? Which was better during that moment of the class? I put the first girl over the second, although next year the second will beat the first because she's soundly grounded in jumping form.

I have gone into this show at some length because I found it a most interesting experience. I also have another reason. I have long felt that in the selection of a judge for Morgan performance classes, it is better to choose someone who is an experienced performance judge, whether or not he knows or cares anything about Morgans, rather than someone who knows Morgans but seldom judges a performance class. The breed class, where the horses are stationary or work out individually, presents much less of a technical problem, as far as I can see. Both men in any class will have to make decisions on the basis of their personal bias, but the other technical problems are solved by the experienced performance judge observing a ring of moving horses. In addition, he knows the gaits and way of going desirable for the class—harness, pleasure, saddle. He often is himself a rider and even an exhibitor. I'd rather take my chances with him, if I cannot have the ideal of the experienced performance judge who also knows Morgans. This, of course, is only my individual opinion.

CHAPTER 15

Odds and Ends of
Life with Horses

I JUST returned from a pleasant horsey mission. I ordered two small wooden plates from a sign maker, marked with my Morgans' names and serial numbers, to dress up my stalls here or at any show I may go to this summer. Bonnie and Jeffy are my horses' stable names, but I use their registered names: Junior Miss and Lord Jeff.

Although I like to buy horse tack, I am not pleased when I must replace a perfectly good all-wool cooler. Jeffy, like the young of all animals, tends to get into things and cause trouble. One rainy day he was shut in the stable. Bored with this confinement he reached over his partition, grabbed Bonnie's lovely green cooler, and apparently spent hours stamping on it with his forefeet while he ripped it into dozens of long streamers with his teeth. It is now being made into a rug. The new cooler should be here any day. I seldom get Bonnie so heated as to need a cooler to walk her in, but I use it quite a lot when she comes in wet with rain. Then I scrape her off and throw the cooler over her until she dries out.

Day after day goes by with no excitement among the livestock, but it pays to keep an eye out. For example, as I was setting the table for dinner one day I saw a smudge of brown flash by the window. It was Jeffy right out straight at top speed chasing a cat out of his pasture. He certainly was breathing down her tail. She slipped under the fence just in the nick of time. To counteract what you are going to think about Jeffy's character after that story, I'll tell you another incident. A small black kitten with a huge voice wandered into our stable when Jeffy was on the floor being groomed. Yelling for food and attention, she wove herself in and out of the four tall black columns of Jeffy's legs. He grew roots from his feet; he did not move an inch. Later I held her up to his face, imprisoning her claws. He closed his usually too busy mouth and gently inhaled the smell of kitten while softly ruffling her fur with a curious nose.

Jeffy is at the stage when he sees the image of the mare in everything—a post, a big rock, a human being, and, of course, Bonnie. It is a little trying but no real problem. When the grass comes up in the pasture it will take up his attention to a large extent. At present I try to give him a little stimulating exercise or at least a fresh branch to play with each day. This solitary state of the stud colt is, of course, quite unnatural. He has Bonnie nearby at least, so he is better off than some.

I find that I become more fond of him as he gets older. He is really a sweet-natured, responsive little colt. The flashes of temper and willfullness that he can show merely give spice to our relationship. I see that I still refer to him as a little colt. This is untrue but reflects the fact that I have known him since he was born. He is actually a big, well-grown horse, massive and powerful. It is fortunate that I still think of him as a baby.

All of us who ride know that a strange object on a familiar route will upset a horse, even a carton by the side of the road. I, at least, had never realized until recently that the absence of a familiar object will also upset a horse. One day I rode Bonnie calmly down our driveway and past the intersection of a grassy lane. Suddenly she spun like a top under me. What was the trouble? Why nothing more than the absence of four jumps that had for months been placed along that lane. Later I drove Jeffy down the same route while he dragged his pine tree. He too spun for the same reason. His spin landed him wedged between two maple saplings where, with the pine tree hitched to him, he could move neither left nor right, forward nor backward. This was one of the occasions when you have to be able to unhitch a colt as smoothly and quickly as possible.

One day a big dead oak that had been a familiar sight here was cut down. It had stood at a distance of over 600 feet from the stable. The next day I let Bonnie out for her turn at the pasture. I heard the thunder of horse hooves and the ringing trumpet of her snort. She was upset by nothing more than the absence of the dead oak. For days afterward, she never entered the pasture without throwing her tail over her back and snorting in the direction where the oak had been.

I used the British caulks on their shoes to prevent slipping on ice for the first time this winter. They are wonderful, well worth their extra price. I have had them on nine weeks now, including a reset of the shoes, and they are still as good as when first put on. My blacksmith says that they are made in Switzerland and sold to this country from England.

I used to hate the job of changing pin caulks. It was necessary to change them between settings of the shoes. Furthermore, even before they had to be changed they would wear down so that the horse stood on an uneven base. It was such hard manual labor to change the caulks that I was tempted to change only those that needed it. Such a procedure still leaves the horse on an uneven base but tipped the other way. With the foreign caulks the chance of a horse caulking itself is remote because the tips are set so low and are so blunt. I used to be afraid to longe Bonnie in the old winter shoes because she gets worked up and does some pretty fancy stepping. I do not hesitate to longe her in these.

CHAPTER 16

*Planning a Small Stable
and Falling Off*

THERE must be a boom in the horse business. In this one small New England town at least six people are trying to buy horses, preferably Morgans. Some of these people are new horse owners. If this is so elsewhere, there must also be a rash of stable construction. Usually I try not to appear to be the voice of experience, since mine is limited. However, on stable construction I do have a few errors to record that you would do well to avoid. In appreciation of our inspired builder, my husband, and also my own plan on graph paper, may I say that we have a nice stable; but little things crop up. It is the little things that I will speak of. The big things— flooring, dimensions of stalls, and so on—anyone can find out by reading, visiting, and talking.

First, high priority in your planning should be given to what you will do with the manure. Plan your stable door and your manure pile in such a way that the quickest and easiest route lies between the two, because it will be a path that you will beat far too often. The three of us thought we had solved that with a very nice indoor pit, opening off a south door from the stable. The trouble was that although the manure went in very easily, it was a Herculean task to get it out again. We now use that for the horses' outdoor shelter and also as a corridor so that I can let the mare out into the pasture without taking her through the stallion's stall. As a result, I have to wheel at least two loads a day almost entirely around the stable to the manure heap.

Point two—where will the snow fall when it melts off the roof? Not, I hope, right in front of your stable door as ours does. Unfortunately, the pitch of our slate roof does not allow an added hood now. Winter also presents a problem from below as well as this one from above—frost heaves. It is not the motorist who knows the full horror of a frost heave. It is the stable owner who at seven in the morning tries to get into his barn to feed the horses. First of all you shovel away the snow that fell off the roof. That is easy. Then you find that the door won't open more than a crack, because the ground has jumped up in the night.

The following is a valid scene. After some struggle I get in the barn. I then go to let Jeffy out by his private door into the pasture. He is eager to get out. He breathes down my neck and practically climbs up my back as I fumble at the latch. I try to swing the door out. It opens only partway, but with liberty in view Jeffy shoves me and himself into the crack. This situation is a first-class booby trap for both of us. I push him back and shut the door again. Then I collect a pickax, a crowbar, and a sledgehammer and go around the other way to hack away enough frozen ground so that I can open his door. This is very bad for the disposition and language. Of course after one such experience a winter, I learn to work at the ground from the outside before even trying to let him out. This could be tragic in case of fire as the horses would be locked in. I hasten to add that we can always get ours out either through the shelter door or through the garage door. So what is the answer? Have sills high enough to take care of the heaving of frozen ground. Our sills are only about an inch, so they should be higher. Wide cement aprons outside the doors would help. Our aprons are only about twenty-four inches wide, and the heave occurs beyond them. Cement must be very scientifically laid or it too can heave. A corner of one of our aprons did heave, and I had to chip that away the first winter. There is not much difference in the work of chipping away cement and that of chipping away frozen ground.

Although our stall floors are a mixture of clay and sand, the aisle is cement. My third point is that it should be rough cement. Ours is as smooth as the floor of a recreation room. This means that now and then I strew sand, if I sense we may have a little excitement on the barn floor. I emphatically do not want either Bonnie or Jeffy to slip and go down. Cement is by no means necessary, but if you are going to use it be sure to specify that it be roughened.

If you are a very new owner you will need to watch out for all sorts of booby traps, whether you have just a wooden shed or a fine brick stable. Make sure the doors the horses use are wide enough so that no part of their tack can catch on anything as they come and go. Eliminate projecting edges where a horse can catch a tie rope or a halter. I remember once feeling that the sky had fallen on me in a stall; and when I came to, there was my horse with a broken halter. She had caught her rope under the edge of her manger at the moment I fed her. She went berserk as they do at such a time and in thrashing around had knocked me out. So much for odds and ends of stable construction. Bonnie and Jeffy and I wish you the best of luck in yours.

A couple of days ago Bonnie and I both bit the dust. The frost had come out of the ground and a stretch of previously perfect sound gravel road was undermined. She has a scratch on her hind leg, and I have a rainbow-hued bicep muscle to show where her nice round knee came down on it. I have fallen from or with horses far too many times to count and so far have had no permanent damage. I'd rather go off a horse than down with one. After forty years of riding I stick much too close to the horse for comfort when we both go down. My first fall at age eleven was with a horse who shied at a car on a slippery road. That time I was flung wide and clear. This time Bonnie and I made just one heap. It is extraordinary how a kindly intentioned and reasonably nimble horse can avoid hurting you with her feet. Bonnie could have put her full weight on my arm and it would surely have broken. She weighs 1,230 pounds.

For just plain throwing me off, the prize goes to one big brute of a horse that threw me three times within one exercise hour in an indoor ring when I was about fourteen. The above is just for some of you who may be new at this game and fear your first fall. You will probably do nothing more serious to yourself than bore your friends with the tale. In fact, I've fallen so many times that I become utterly relaxed and in about forty years have never ended up in a doctor's office. One caution, don't put your arm out to save yourself; hang onto the reins. That keeps your arms up and you don't have to walk home. I learned this from an ex-cavalry officer at age eleven in Oxford, England.

CHAPTER 17

The Jogging Cart

I WRITE this on the last day of January 1953. Jeffy, my bay Morgan stallion, is nineteen months and seventeen days old. He stands a little over fourteen and a half hands high and is sufficiently massive to wear Bonnie's horse-size harness. He has graduated in his schooling and started on his life's work. In short, he is harness broken. I will not go so far as to say that he is harness trained, but he knows all about three different kinds of things to pull. He accepts as a matter of course more items of harness than he will need later. He knows how to pull his strength and his weight into his shoulders and pull and likewise to push back into a breeching. To do him full justice he seemed to know all this at once, the very first day he was hitched to a cart. He has never reared, kicked, thrown himself, or even fussed. It all seemed to come quite naturally to him. To be sure, his early attitude of almost solemn quietness has been superseded, with growing confidence, by a rather cocky air and a tendency to get a bit above himself with consequent problems of handling to this inexperienced driver.

My early foolishness one night with a self-made so-called travois was a mistake reported in chapter 13. What did I do, therefore, to bring about this happy result? First I decided that I would not use makeshift rigs concocted from raids on Toby's toolbox and lumber. A friend gave me an old-fashioned, very high wheeled jogging cart with bucket seats and stirrups. I had this thoroughly overhauled by professionals. It is light as a feather, perfect for Jeffy, and for me,

63

Jeffy now stands over fourteen
hands high and is sufficiently
massive for horse-size harness,
January 1953.

Early lessons in driving. Jeffy is
learning to pull a small tree,
February 1953.

Jeffy now knows the basics of
harness work and is ready for
more advanced training, March
1953.

since I sit so high I can see every flick of his ear. Next I swallowed my pride and called in the very best and most experienced man I know of to help. I shall call him Dick since he lives down the road a piece and is my neighbor. He is very well known for his success with young horses through his quiet, calm competence.

Before doing that, however, Toby, Billy, and I accustomed Jeffy to the cart. I drove him in long reins while the men pulled the cart first on one side and then on the other and lastly so that the shafts embraced Jeffy in the position they would be if hitched. We thus drove him on grass, gravel, and macadam to accustom him to the sound of the metal rims. This seemed completely pointless since at no time did Jeffy object, but I am sure that it was useful. We did this in three lessons.

It is apparently very important that a young horse never takes fright and successfully runs away in harness. I was afraid I had marked Jeffy's mind already from the night misadventure, but possibly because I had not let him get away, it had no bad effect on him.

When he was first hitched to the cart, Dick had Billy hold loosely a lead strap to a halter under his bridle on the off side, while Dick himself held one on the near side and I drove him from the ground. We went around the pasture and out on the road. For the next lesson, I rode on the cart and Dick held a longe line. That time Jeffy trotted. He was also asked to stop short many times to engage the breeching and to turn sharply for the pressure of the shafts. After that, with Toby's help or alone, I drove him in the pasture. Then Dick showed me a method often used as a first step in harness breaking, that is, to have the colt pull a small felled tree. We tied a small pine to a whiffletree and the traces to the whiffletree. These ties must be able to be unfastened instantly. We used short lengths of baling string. I later discovered how instantly and how often the traces have to be freed, so I used short lengths of chain with an open hook that is easier to undo with gloves on in cold weather. A colt by whirling or backing can really get snarled up in that arrangement. I use it quite a lot without anyone else to help.

The advantage of the contraption is that a colt gets the feeling of the traces inside and outside of his legs and also learns to stand quietly and let man free him from any predicament he gets into. After a few lessons in driving to the cart or tree, Dick came again to hitch him for the first time to the sleigh. My sleigh is heavy, but Jeffy was not downhearted; he just pulled that much harder.

None of these lessons have been over a half hour in length. For all of them he wore a kicking as a precaution. As a more necessary measure he wears a loose bearing rein side check to stop him dropping his head for a really good buck or plunge from playfulness, a tendency that becomes more pronounced as the lessons progress. His bridle is open so that he can see me and the vehicle. His increasing playfulness results from confidence, snappy weather, and a vital spirit fed by plenty of grain. For these reasons I have not driven him on the road by myself.

I am right on my planned schedule for his education. He is harness broken by his second winter. I shall do little driving now until spring and then put him through a more concentrated course. I plan no saddle work until his third fall, when he will be two and a half.

Both horses were immunized as permanently as possible against tetanus. A few years ago Bonnie pulled a shoe partway off and then stepped back onto an exposed nail. I had her given a tetanus antitoxin shot then. Since Jeffy frequently nicks himself, I decided I would get them both fixed up so that I could forget the tetanus problem.

Jeffy has a behavior problem apparently not uncommon to bored, solitary colts. He has spells of spinning around and around trying to bite his hocks or his stifles, first one way and then the other. It does no harm and with the stimulus of training and the consequent exercise it seems to decrease. After he is gelded and can have Bonnie to play with, I think he will really be a more contented colt.

CHAPTER 18

The Pros and Cons of Gelding

THE doctor came during the past month of May to geld Jeffy. I felt like a traitor when I arranged it, but at the same time I felt that it was the right thing to do. The operation is done under anesthesia. Convalescence for a two-year-old colt should be no problem. Some of you owners of colts must be facing this decision right now.

Situated as we are, and with my lack of time and experience, I would not keep a stud here for breeding. Therefore, I had never considered keeping Jeffy a stallion. If I had intended to sell him, I could have done so as a yearling stallion. Now at two years of age, he could bring a higher price gelded, harness trained, and started under saddle after next fall. He would be too young yet to have proven his breeding worth. The value of a sire is not only in his own conformation and performance but even more so in that of his average children from many different mares. It takes more than a decade to reveal the quality of a sire. Good as Jeffy's heredity is, there is no scarcity of his line. His grand-champion sire has years of activity before him. His half brother is also a grand champion. His relatives crop up everywhere from both sides of his family. He is not the end of a vanishing line that should be preserved.

Some people like to have a stallion for a pleasure horse. I found that even the kind, two-year-old Jeffy caused so much extra trouble and concern that it was not worth it. I always had to think about the security of gates, doors, fences. Later my concern would have included the other horses that we ride with and their riders. I would have had to be very sure that I could stick with him under all circumstances. There was nothing mean about Jeffy, but he was strong, vigorous, and full of stallion ardor. I could let Bonnie loose around the place here to graze on the choice hay land but not Jeffy. He had to make do on the worn-out grass of the pasture, unless I led him out and held him while he grazed.

From his point of view, if I may presume to see it, I feel that the gelding's greater liberty and naturalness in life-style more than offset the temporary discomfort of the operation. Now, after gelding, he is not hedged in with prohibitions and cautions. If he gets loose, no one needs to be concerned except for the usual hazards. He can share in the close companionship of other horses, which only the wild range stallion can do. Horses are gregarious; they like to be together.

If I had another colt and it was reasonably well developed in the spring of its yearling stage, I think I would geld it then. This second year has given Jeffy a fine chest and crest, but he might have had them anyway. It has been a bother to care for him with the restrictions mentioned above. May was apparently the month to choose for the operation. The weather settled down to warm and dry, and the flies weren't too bad.

This spring I drove him a good deal by myself but only around the place. He is much better behaved. He has, to a large extent, stopped fooling around and trying to play. Both horses came through the winter in wonderful shape. They are fat and sleek. I took Bonnie's shoes off for a month while we were in Florida and later. She had no exercise except from random movements in the pasture. As a result, when I started to work her she was soft and lazy, puffing at the least exertion. She has hardened up now with short, almost daily, rides or drives and proportionately less roughage in her diet. By the end of April I started her over very low jumps as I had done the previous spring.

Recently I had one of those stable accidents that are an occupational hazard to those who deal with horses. I never dreamed that Jeffy would think that a new saddle smelled like a dead pig or that a saddle would be any different to him than a harness saddle, which he has worn dozens of times. I had a new saddle I wanted to try on him for size and especially size of girth, which I knew was too short for Bonnie. He had never worn a saddle and wouldn't be worked in one until next fall. I cross-tied him, cleaned him off, and went into the house for the saddle without the slightest inkling of an idea of trouble. Before I even reached the open barn door I heard the plunging sounds of an upset horse. Either the squeak of the new leather or a whiff of it had reached him. I held it out for him to smell. "No, no, no, take it away," he said as clearly as words as he rushed forward, backward, and sideways to the limit of the new strong cross-ties. Oh, dear, I had started something and must now see it through. I got Bonnie's old saddle. Ah, that was better. After about ten minutes of soft talk from me, and restless sniffing and fidgeting on his part, I slipped it on his back and girthed it up. I left it there for a while and scratched his neck and made much of him. So far so good, but I still had to get that new saddle on. After about a half hour of nonsense on his part, including actual trembling when the saddle touched him, he calmed down and I quietly slid it on his back. Bang! He slammed me against the blanket rail and pinned me there. Hardly able to breathe, I said, "Ssh, ssh, there, there, it is all right," and moved him over with a touch on the flank. I did it a second time, and for a second time I was pinned against the rail. This time, he stood quietly after he released me and I could try the girth. It was much too short. I couldn't buckle it at all. There, that was how big "little" Jeffy was. At the age of two he had to have an outsized girth, like his mother. The moral of this story is to be sure to measure new tack before you oil and can't return it; also, that a colt may not like the smell of new leather, no matter how much he has worn old leather. Now a bouquet for Jeffy. If ever a colt had a reason to strike, Jeffy had it there. Not once did he raise a forefoot except to move. To be sure, in his fear and desperation he pinned me against the wall, but he freed me each time on signal. Good little Jeffy. I should never have started this, but how did I know it was going to mean trouble?

CHAPTER 19

The Operation, Driving

TODAY Jeffy is two years and ten days old. He stands nearly fifteen hands, one inch and is a well-developed bright bay with black legs, mane, and tail. Within the last month he passed two major milestones in his life's path. He was gelded and had his first shoeing. Neither event seemed to upset him in the least.

What sort of a journal would this be if I made no reference to Our Operation! The doctor, his assistant, and Dick took Jeffy out into the pasture. There he was blindfolded, given an anesthetic, and by a throwing harness laid down on the grass. Since I am not one for operations, I busied myself making up a deep bed of clean straw in his stall, which I had previously washed with a disinfectant. I had hardly finished when back came the procession. I had expected a pretty downcast, if not sick, colt. Quite the contrary, with bright and shining eye, he at once fell to on his hay. I had withheld food since the night before, and he was ravenously hungry. Well, that was all there was to it. I kept him in that day and night. Next morning I washed him off and started to give him the gentle exercise the doctor had recommended that he have in the morning and in the evening. I led him out for what I presumed would be a quiet stroll, but he was such a little demon, I turned him loose. He reared, wheeled, and shot off across the pasture. Thereafter he exercised himself abundantly. At least once every day something would stimulate him, and he would run and buck and rear, all of his own volition. At no time did he display any discomfort or

71

reluctance to move. The only precaution I took was to keep him as clean as possible to avoid infection. I kept his stall clean all the time, and I shut him out of the paddock where much of the ground is bare. He was either loose in the sod-covered pasture or in his stall.

In about a week he calmed down and I started to drive him again. Almost at once I had an unfortunate training mishap. I was unhitching him one day and had reached the point when he was almost free of the cart but not quite. He moved, the cart responded in a strange way, and he took fright and was off. I grabbed for the reins and caught only one. This one I clung to. Thus held on one side he wheeled through the lilacs, the cart loosely and awkwardly flapping behind him, scaring him more. I fell and was dragged on my stomach. The loose shaft of the cart went right over his back, and the cart tipped over and was finally freed from the still-fastened wrap strap. As a dead weight on one side of his mouth, I brought him around a second time through the lilacs, and there he stopped. Damage consisted of a broken seat on the cart, a small scratch on me, and two badly shaken up nervous systems—Jeffy's and mine. I was in a yellow funk about ever hitching him up again alone. I am here alone all day. Toby has his work to do. I have to hitch him alone.

The first thing I did was to see my neighbor, Dick, and beg his help. He came the next morning and three more times. This restored Jeffy's confidence in the unhitching process. Dick also drove him for me on the road over the railroad tracks, bridges, and past cattle and dogs. Jeffy recovered from his fright but I did not. I have no good place to cross-tie while hitching. The garage floor is the only possibility and that is smooth as glass to slip on. Furthermore, the top of the overhead door is so low that Jeffy could easily crack his head on it with one good toss. I tried cross-tying him there to groom one day and he promptly pulled back and broke his tie ropes, although he is always cross-tied to groom in the stable. My mentor does not approve of cross-tying colts to hitch anyway. They must learn to stand.

One morning, using Toby's eye through the breakfast room window as a challenge and a support, I hitched him according to a plan I had developed. It worked perfectly. I have been hitching him by myself now for two weeks. This is what I do. I roll the cart into the paddock and leave it with the shafts facing Jeffy's private Dutch door into the same area. Harnessed, I lead him out of this door and turn him so that he faces in toward his stall with the lower part of the door closed and the upper part open. He is thus walled in from the front. On his left is the paddock fence, on his right the open top half of his stall door. Taking all the time I want, I hitch him, get in the cart, back him, and turn and go out the gate. To unhitch I do the same thing in reverse. It works very well.

A friend recommended that I drive him several miles a day so that he will not get above himself. This serves also to muscle him up and acquaint him with the sights and sounds about the town. In our location, this means trotting on macadam. The vet, a horseman himself, recommended rubber shoes so that he would not slip during one of his frequent shies and to ease the concussion of the hard road. Jeffy has at present excellent feet, and I want to keep them that way. While he has the rubber shoes this month, I will drive him a lot on the macadam. Then for the show I will change to steel. Later, saddle work can start, and I think I will remove his shoes again until next spring. The first shoeing was apparently insignificant to Jeffy. He made no fuss at all. For a couple of weeks before the blacksmith came, I tapped his hooves all around the edges each time I cleaned them.

As a gelding now, Jeffy is allowed to reach Bonnie across the fence. I removed the aisle that separated them. They are both so happy with the smell and taste of each other. They stand one on each side of the fence, lapping and lapping each other on the neck and shoulder. I have not put them together yet because both are shod and because Bonnie, in training for jumping, should not have as much grass as Jeffy may. Except for about an hour in the pasture, she has the barren paddock and he has the pasture.

Jeffy's greater contentment and peace is seen in other ways. He has, for example, stopped spinning around to bite his stifles. In our relations the most marked change is that I, or anyone else, can go into his pasture at any time without his instant, passionate attendance. As a stallion he would come up at once, without malice, nipping, threatening to rear on you, talking stud talk, and generally being a nuisance. Now he may come up, but it is only from serene inquisitiveness, not from his past driving, restless force.

Jeffy and Bonnie . . . so happy with the smell and taste of each other.

CHAPTER 20

Showing Bonnie and Jeffy

I HAVE been asked quite often how long I can keep this journal going. Sometimes I wonder, too. However, I am writing about living animals in changing conditions, which is far easier than to have to depend on inspiration and research for the subject matter. At this time I have on hand a number of subjects for the future, if nothing more vital arises—Jeffy and the driving problem, Bonnie, the jumper, second edition revised, Bonnie, the equitation horse. For today, however, I want to write about showing horses, because that is a subject that will be easiest for me and most timely right now. As I write this I gaze with great pleasure at a silver trophy and a blue, red, and yellow ribbon won by Jeffy and Bonnie last weekend.

I will tell what I do to prepare for showing, but I hope that none of you think that I necessarily recommend the same for you and your horses. To some of you my doings may seem fussy, to the big-time exhibitor my methods will seem casual. I am not writing for them. I am writing for those of you new to showing that you may have some idea of what may be involved. My philosophy is that if I show at all my horses and my tack must be in as good show condition as my time, experience, and money can provide. You see, there are three qualifications there that limit my showing conditions.

My first show this year was at the end of July and the first of August. Bonnie and Jeffy came through the winter in fine shape, thanks in part to the control of bloodworms, with

Jeff competing as a two-year-old gelding at the National Morgan Horse Show, July 31, 1954.

which my land seems to be infected. I had, therefore, no building-up process to go through this spring.

Food and exercise come first in getting into show condition. Starting about the middle of June, I began to drive Jeffy about two or three miles a day, partly at the walk and partly at the trot. Likewise Bonnie, who had been casually hacked all spring about four times a week, began to get light, almost daily, exercise either under saddle or on the longe with the rare inclusion of a very few low jumps. Such an increase in exercise built muscle but required an increase in food to maintain flesh. As Bonnie's grain went up slightly, her hay and grass were cut because I belong to the school that does not believe in jumping and galloping on a stomach loaded with bulky foods. At night, however, she had all the hay she wanted. Bonnie's breathing at the gallop tells me that my method works best with her. Jeffy, who was not supposed to do any fast work, could still have all the grass and hay he wanted to grow on. Since every horse's food requirement has to be figured out individually, there is no point going into quantities. I will merely say that two quarts of crimped oats with one quart of bran is the basic diet fed morning and afternoon with light exercise. From that I build up under conditions of more exercise and may lower under certain circumstances. In winter I substitute some horse feed, and the colt gets some most of the year. When Jeffy was younger he got much more than this, up to nine quarts a day in three feedings. The quality of the hay also affects the amount of grain fed. The problem seems to me to be that of building muscle without losing flesh.

One of the best ways to lose flesh, beside running it off, is to allow flies to fret it off. Both horses, except during work, therefore, were confined to the stable during the heat of the day. Jeffy had the run of the pasture all night; Bonnie had it for an hour or two in the very early morning. My horses tell me clearly that they like this system. They do not want to be fly bitten and scorched in the sun. They love to be out at night and in the early dewy morning. This also preserves their coats from the drying and bleaching action of the sun.

Under this system of food and exercise I got along into

July. Bonnie began to feel pretty good in her quiet way. She moved freer, was better balanced, and livelier. One day she even bolted just for the fun of it. This light daily exercise conditioned her and did not wear her out. I started to ride her over the jumps, instead of jumping her free, and took longer gallops. Since she got above my basic grain ration, I gave her a warm bran and linseed mash without oats about once a week before a day of rest. Jeffy adores this, but he only gets to lick the spoon, because his growth can take care of any excess protein in the grain. So he continues on his diet of somewhat above the basic ration. You realize that I am speaking only of conditioning a mare for pleasure and jumping classes and a colt for model. For what I call the peacock classes, bitting harness and ring work would be the form of exercise.

I cannot here, for lack of space, say anything about training, except that I find some ring work even for pleasure classes necessary. I also find it important to train for the exact requirements of the class, for example, drive, ride, and jump two obstacles. I did just that twice before the show with my already-trained mare. Since I could not get my temporary ring up until ten days before the show, I did not start ring work until then. Jeffy was led out there, walked and trotted in hand on the line, and set up for a model about five times. He has been trained in this long ago, so these were just rehearsals.

Now to consider external appearances. The health and condition of the horses had given their coats a natural gleam. About two weeks before the show I rolled up my sleeves and really groomed them, instead of my customary brush-off. All sorts of shortcuts to success are suggested for this business; but in my conservative, old-fashioned way, I find no substitute for the standard implements and lots of elbow grease used daily. While the horses were in the stable I kept a sheet on them. Within the last week I trimmed their legs to remove the long hairs, which gives that neat and tidy look. Hand clippers do this well, but I was lazy this year and borrowed electric clippers. With curved-blade fetlock scissors I removed the long hairs around and in the ears and trimmed

Jeff is the winner of "Model Gelding, Two Years Old," at the National Morgan Horse Show, July 31, 1954.

up the place behind the ears where the bridle goes. I did not trim the long hairs around the eyes, which are protective. On the day before the show, I trimmed off the whiskers around the mouth and washed the mane, tail, legs, and face. Billy came to help that day and to give the final polish to their coats. I found that once I get to a show, I can never clean the horses as well as I can at home. On or before this last day, the tack was thoroughly cleaned and packed up.

About two weeks before the show the blacksmith came to shoe Bonnie and trim Jeffy. The doctor also came and gave them both a shot to protect against various catching ills that beset horses in traveling and showing.

Once at the show grounds the first thing Bill and I did was to go over every foot of the stalls and remove the odd nails and projections that racehorse handlers install in their horses' homes. We then put chain and snap fasteners on the doors since the little wooden blocks that are the usual fixtures, if any are present at all, seem to be child's play to my horses to open. Last year Jeffy burst off five of them, so now we take no chances. We put a good stout block at the bottom, which they cannot reach and will hold the door if they start banging away with their front feet. We also screwed in rings to hang the water buckets on. My horses are used to a constant water supply, unless hot, and to change their habits at the show would be to invite trouble. Having spread straw, we installed the horses, gave them water and hay, and hoped they would settle down. Bonnie did so at once. Jeffy wanted to leave by any method as soon as possible, so for about a half hour Billy stayed there with him holding his lead strap. In that time he too settled down and started to enjoy himself. He loved the show and had a marvelous time.

Overnight and most of the day, Bill stayed with the horses. Except for one show, I have always had someone stay with the horses all night. Bill slept in the trailer right outside their stalls. In case of fire he could get them out. In case of illness he could get expert help. Bill is only fourteen, but he is very dependable and gets along very well with horses. Even as a sassy little stud, Jeffy never caused him any trouble. That then is the story until the time when the great show opened.

CHAPTER 21

∽∽∽∽∽∽∽∽∽∽∽∽∽∽∽∽∽∽∽∽∽∽∽∽∽

Saddle Education

A T the age of two years and three months Jeffy was first backed, that is, saddled and sat upon. This momentous event happened about two weeks ago and was no sudden thing; it took about a week of saddle introduction before I threw my leg over and sat astride.

You may remember that last March Jeffy made quite a dustup because I innocently tried a new saddle on him for size, expecting no trouble at all and receiving plenty. Hence, when his age and strength were right, according to my theory, for first saddle education, I went at it very gradually. I spent about a week in preliminaries. First I put an English saddle on the straw in his stall while I groomed him. He smelled it and pulled it about by the stirrup leathers. The next day I rubbed it over him as he stood in his stall tied to the manger. Then I gently slipped it on his back first from one side and then the other. On the fourth day, I put it on and girthed him up and left him saddled for about an hour.

At any new operation his head goes up and his ears turn back toward the saddle. He appears to be listening to an inner voice from his instincts and his reflexes. Apparently thus assured that all is well, he relaxes. For the next three days I added outdoor work by longeing him in the saddle, first with the stirrups off and later pulled down to slap against his side and shoulder. On the same days, work in the stall continued. I put pressure and weight first on one stirrup and then on the other. I became more casual in placing the saddle and rougher in snapping the stirrups against the flaps. Then

81

quietly I raised myself to lie across the saddle, first from one side, then the other. Lastly I raised myself slowly and sank down astride in the saddle. Thus was Jeffy backed.

For a few days more I continued work in the big box stall—mounting from both sides with increasing casualness, vaulting off to either side. I even rode him there to teach him to turn his haunches with the touch of the leg on one side, then on the other, and to move forward with the pressure of both.

All stall work was done with only a halter on him so he would not be distracted from the saddle by a bit. Whether or not these precautions pay off remains to be seen. None of them are original with me. The use of the home stall is a well-accepted practice, both because it gives a sense of security to the colt and because it is too familiar to distract. Practice in all things from both near and off side of the horse is standard procedure.

For three days I have been riding him in a snaffle bridle in the paddock. None of these lessons except longeing have been over fifteen minutes. With my unaccustomed weight, he walks with tentative steps. He knows already the elementary leg aids. Only at the end of today's lesson did he take his first confident bold step. All too soon, I fear, will come his cocky phase. I have also hand-grazed him and turned him loose in the pasture saddled because I want him to feel at home when saddled but free of control. That leads me to Jeffy and the driving problem.

You may have noticed that I have not mentioned Jeffy, the harness horse, lately. Furthermore, I did not mention in the last chapter that he did not appear in the two-year-old driving class. Jeffy ran in harness and got away from me. In about five minutes he created enough damage, except to himself, the cart, harness, and myself, to make work for Toby for a full day. He went through two jumps, a barbed-wire fence, a grape trellis, he broke a sparrow hawk nesting box on a twelve-foot pole and a hummingbird feeder, as well as assorted vegetation, and lowered the milk production of twelve guernsey cows. Finally, he called forth in Toby a genius for sitting on a horse's head. You may smile, but it was no joke at the time, as at least a dozen haymakers can attest.

All this havoc occurred after at least a month of uneventful, almost daily, drives and after a half hour of calm driving in and out and around the working haying machinery and scattered bales. What can have caused it? I did something I had never had occasion to do before. I got off the cart to fix his rein, which had got caught around the shaft as he switched his head at a fly. It was while I was still on the ground preparing to remount that he took off. What lies back of it? Possibly a sort of panic resulting from a sense of freedom while hitched, as one book suggests. Someone said that the fact that he was thrown by a harness for gelding might have this effect. Others deny it. The earlier incident I wrote up may be the background for this; that happened again while I was on the ground unhitching. That time I held him, however. This then is the problem. Except for one thing I am letting the solution ride a while. Driving was delayed in any case for needed repairs to the cart and harness, so I am going ahead with saddle work at this time.

The one measure I have taken on the problem is to longe him with the severe and secure control of a chain over the nose from the web line instead of the easier padded metal nosepiece of my standard longeing caveson. I started soon after the runaway and worked him briefly almost every day for about two weeks. On the very first day he gave me the chance I was hoping for. He had walked and trotted calmly both ways. Just before putting him away I let him walk just a little more to cool him out. He couldn't have been better mannered. Suddenly I saw his whole body sink toward the ground, then like a released springboard he was off. I was ready for him and I snapped the line twice just as hard as I could. That did it. He stopped dead in his tracks. The next four days he tried to run at least once each day, but his heart was no longer in it. These runs were tests of me and my intentions. He has always repeated his wicked behavior to try me out. Never again after those first four days has he run on the longe. I hope very much that this will turn out like his rearing phase at the age of about seven months. Then it took about four days of consistent punishment for each rear before he gave up. He has never reared since either in hand, in harness, or under saddle.

I was amused at Bonnie today. She was in the pasture as I rode Jeffy in the paddock. At once she noticed it and came running over to the fence talking to Jeffy. She would have paid no attention if he had been in hand or in harness for she is well accustomed to those sights.

Jeffy's saddle education progresses smoothly. He graduated from early lessons in his boxstall, to the paddock, and from there to the pasture. I started about the middle of August when he was two years and two months old. It is now the second week in October. Lessons were interrupted for about two weeks until the day before yesterday. I noticed that he started out again with the same hesitancy of his early rides, but yesterday he moved more freely.

I try to follow the advice in *Training Hunters, Jumpers and Hacks* by Harry D. Chamberlain. This British book by a U.S. Cavalry officer is a classic on training for these purposes. I chose this way because it uses the methods and achieves the results that I am best acquainted with. There are certainly other ways. I know that the hackamore, for example, can produce very good results and I thought of trying it. However, to do so seemed silly since I have never ridden with a hackamore, so I would be adding my ignorance to Jeffy's.

Many people in this country consider the bitting harness essential to producing correct head carriage, especially for showing. At every show you see very fine results obtained by hours of careful and experienced use of a bitting harness, but I am not practiced in the use of this device. For the unskilled there are dangers, chiefly that of the horse not learning to go into his bridle and accept the bit. I also do not much care for a rigidity, especially a lateral stiffness, that some horses trained in the bitting harness acquire. I like a pleasure horse to be supple and pliant from side to side and head to tail.

In riding Jeffy I try to push him with my legs down a funnel formed by the two reins of the snaffle bit, which I hold well separated in each hand. This discourages his coltish tendency to veer from side to side and encourages him to go into his bridle, as it is said. At each walking step, I let my hands follow the nod of his head so as not to jar his mouth.

For a long time, he has known that a pressure on his side means to move his haunches away from that side. Therefore, the use of each leg separately makes sense to him, but he has no idea what both together mean. To make him move forward, I have to cluck or tap him with a stick while I close my legs. He is now getting the idea of that. We walk chiefly as fast as I can push him, which is not yet very fast, turn in circles and right angles, start, and stop. Toward the end we trot a bit. So far he has not put up any bad resistance.

For a while he was a little reluctant to leave the barn, but a few light swats got him over that. He often tried to put his head way down and jog me in a circle back to the barn, but that too has passed. He gave a couple of mild bucks and kicks but nothing to threaten to unseat me. To his great credit, he stands like a rock to mount and dismount. I think that my frequent early mountings in his stall helped on this. There was no place to go, so why move. Once in the saddle, I take a lot of time on purpose—feeling the girth, adjusting the stirrups, or just sitting. I don't want him to get the idea he should move the minute I land in the saddle.

I am strongly tempted to go out on the road. However, there is only one good training excuse for this now. It would give him longer straightaways to develop a fast walk. To offset this advantage are the varied sights and sounds to distract him from the things I am trying to tell him with my hands and legs. No, I shall try to force myself to stay in the pasture for at least a month.

Jeffy has quite a different feel under me from Bonnie. He is a better Morgan because he is more compact. In comparison with Bonnie, there doesn't seem to be much horse either in front of me or behind me—it is all underneath. Although he is nearly as tall and takes almost as much girth, I can easily reach his ears and his tail from the saddle, which I cannot with Bonnie. Bonnie's graceful, crested neck is untypically long for a Morgan, but I like it because it is the kind of neck that I was brought up to think a horse should have (I am a Johnny-come-lately to Morgans). It gives plenty of rein in front of me. He differs in another way; his trot is very easy to sit to without posting. Bonnie's trot is jumpy so it is easier

85

to post. So much for little Jeffy at this time. He is a good boy and I am pleased with him.

One of my readers wrote and asked what to do about her horse that shies at papers and cartons. Lots of horses with more sense will shy just for the fun of it, if they are feeling gay. I had a three-quarter black thoroughbred for a while, who on certain days would shy like a youngster at everything, even though she was old enough to vote. However, it might help our correspondent's horse to expose it to lots of blowing papers and cardboard boxes. For Jeffy's education I twice separated all the pages of a Sunday paper and let them blow about his pasture. Naturally I did not do this in any way to frighten him. I released the papers a long ways from him, at first anyway, and then let him explore their dangers on his own the rest of the day. He would sneak up on a moving sheet, ears and nostrils aquiver, and finally take it in his teeth and shake it. I did the same with fertilizer bags and cartons. He tears them to pieces with his teeth until bored, but I have never seen him eat any. I suppose it might be well to watch for that. Now he pays no attention to such things. I keep meaning to accustom him to umbrellas: I must do it before I get caught sometime as an umbrella can really upset a horse.

I was shocked to read the other day of a little girl who lost her life by being dragged by a runaway horse. If any parents or young people new to horses are reading this, I wish you would go out in the barn and look at your English saddle before you forget. An English saddle should have a safety bar with a catch on the end. The catch is to stop the stirrup leather coming off when your legs go back in the saddle. This arrangement, unless the catch is rusted shut (which it often is), will release the leather of the stirrup with a backward pull and thus release a thrown rider whose foot is stuck in the stirrup. This is a very important device. If your saddle does not have a safety bar, a harness maker can put one on. I ride all the time with the catch open. As a result I sometimes have the stirrup leather fall off, but so far I have never gone with the stirrup. At shows, haven't you seen a whole stirrup come off, leather and all? That is the safety bar doing its job with a little more thoroughness than necessary. A western saddle with an enclosed box stirrup is free of this danger. Another safeguard is to learn to hold to the reins when you are thrown until you are sure you are free of the horse. That is what I was taught at the age of eleven, and several hundred people can testify that when thrown at a show, I freeze to the reins. It is not necessary to be as tenacious as I was. On the other hand, I certainly wouldn't have had to walk home on my own two feet if I had been thus dumped in the wide open spaces.

CHAPTER 22

~~~~~~

The Safety Bar

"PRIDE goeth before a fall." In the last chapter I wrote that I had never fallen when the stirrup leather came off the safety bar. Since then I did fall and demonstrated to all the spectators at a small local gymkhana how a safety bar works on an English saddle. Bonnie and I were in the open jumping class. We entered at a walk, quietly circled, and headed for the first jump. On the descent from the jump, my right foot seemed to leave me and threatened to take the whole of me to the ground. Confound it, the stirrup leather came off the safety bar at the very first jump! I would be disqualified if I stopped to put it back on or if I fell off before completing the course. Naturally I tried to ride it out. I took my left foot out of the stirrup for better balance. Then as I bucketed about on top, Bonnie took the course, did it clean, and won the blue. I survived on top just long enough to get past the last jump and then fell off.

Great credit goes to Bonnie for this performance. Although the jumps were very low, I guess nothing over two feet six, they had four things wrong with them to cause a horse to refuse or run out. First of all, they called for a counterclockwise course, that is, a jump off a left lead. The traditional course and the one for which jumpers are largely trained is clockwise. Second, they were very narrow, inviting a run-out, as indeed most of the horses did. Third, they were not even against the rail, as well as being wingless, so that a horse could run out either left or right. Lastly, the nature of the jumps was an insult to a horse. They had only one cross-bar and that a little piece of lathlike wood. A horse jumps much better if he respects the jump for its look of solidness.

Now although Bonnie was a very good girl, I don't want you to think that she or any horse so helplessly ridden would have done that from chance and goodwill alone. No, indeed, I gave Bonnie hours of training for jumping. I started by leading her over a series of logs laid on the ground and gradually progressed to jumping three feet absolutely free (no rider, no longe, both clockwise and counterclockwise) and ended with jumping under saddle over all sorts of obstacles to somewhat over three feet. So once in that gymkhana ring with those tiny little jumps, all I had to do was to see that she was headed for the center of the jump, give her her head, and then, stirrup-less, pray that I would stick with her over it. I must practice staying on top of a horse over jumps without stirrups. This loss of stirrup can happen anytime.

When you have once been a teacher the temptation to sound off is very strong, and I cannot resist making some remarks about my fellow competitors in that class. Despite the direction of the course and the nature of the jumps, they were so very low that every single one of my competitors should have been able to do them clean or at least have the horse try willingly. As it happens, I only remember one other even trying the whole course without a refusal or a run-out. If the horses had had a little of the quiet basic training that Bonnie had and if they had not been ridden in curb bits alone, they should have tried the course willingly. The reason they were in curb bits was that almost all were in western tack. I have never seen a horse seriously jumped in a curb bit used alone. It is much worse to practice a green horse in a curb bit.

To see the reason for this, imagine that you yourself are jumping a barrier. As you jump you throw one arm out in front of you. This seems to help lift you over. Afraid to throw out your arm, or with it tied down, you could not jump as well. A horse throws his head and neck out, just as you throw your arm. On top of the jump he reaches out his head to the full stretch of his neck and lowers it. This transfers his weight forward and frees his hind end from it. Thus, he can more easily lift his hind legs to clear the bar. This freeing of his hind end from weight is more successful if you, the rider, also help by using the forward seat, which is impossible in a western saddle where the horn prevents your getting forward over his neck. The trouble with a curb bit is that it is a severe bit and a horse does not willingly go into it. A jumping horse is afraid to make that bold stretch of his neck so necessary for a good jump. A green jumper practiced in a curb (a curb would never be used to train for jumping, so I used the word practiced) has unquestionably been snatched up on it, and so he is afraid of it and learns to refuse the jump entirely. Why unquestionably? Because an untrained horse can do very odd and uncomfortable gymnastics getting over a jump, which will throw the rider, unless very good indeed, back in his saddle. This causes a shortening of the reins and a quite unconscious snatch at the mouth and has nothing whatever to do with the height of the jump. To an untrained horse eighteen inches is as three feet to a trained one. That is why jump height should be raised very gradually in training.

By far and away the best bit to jump in is a thick, jointed snaffle, which is the most comfortable of all bits. The next best, if more control is needed, is a Pelham, being careful not to use the curb part at the moment of the leap itself. Of course, if you are very, very good indeed and riding a well-trained jumper, you would jump the horse on contact, that is, with contact to his mouth through the reins. Far wiser for unsure riders, and especially when riding an untrained jumper, is to give his head complete freedom and even grab a hunk of mane during the jump itself. In this way you are protecting his mouth from a snatch and encouraging him to make that forward swing of his head and neck. If you are riding bareback or in an English saddle, get your weight forward and thus in all ways help him just as much as you can.

The red-ribbon winner demonstrated nicely the effect of a curb. I doubt that the rider even knew why the horse knocked down the bar, but the spectator could see it. This horse took all the jumps boldly. On one jump, at the point where he should have stretched his neck and lowered his head, he tossed it up in reaction to the curb. This brought his weight back toward the rear, his hindquarters dropped where they should have risen, and down went the bar.

Young Jeffy is doing very well under saddle. We have now graduated to the open, although I still start the ride in the pasture to rehearse responses to leg and hand. So far he has never made an effort with the sole aim of unseating me; however, I can't sleep in the saddle because he moves like lightning if startled by something. Following Colonel Chamberlain's advice, I am riding him with very short, blunt dummy spurs. This is no reflection on a horse's spirit, but any young saddle horse must learn to move forward promptly at the will of the rider, shown by just a closing of the legs. I use them very seldom, but if he does not move at once when I close my legs, or move his haunch promptly to one side when I use one leg, then I turn my toe out to bring the metal against his side right behind the girth. After a few days his responses were so much quicker that I now hardly need them. Chamberlain is writing of training thoroughbreds; no one questions the spirit of a thoroughbred, any more than I question Jeffy's. It is just a matter of having that spirit serve the rider's wishes rather than those of the horse.

CHAPTER 23

∽∿∽∿∽∿∽∿∽∿∽∿∽∿∽∿∽∿∽∿∽∿∽∿∽∿∽∿∽∿∽∿∽

The Sun Trap and
Further Training

AS I write this, a fine powdery snow blows in horizontal streaks before a north wind. It is the first real snow of the season. The horses, which I had let out at about nine o'clock, are back in the barn again after an hour or so of quarreling over possession of the sun trap. The sun trap is a small corner in the paddock protected by the wall of the stable, the shelter, and a high palisade fence. It is open to the sky and to the south. There is plenty of room for two horses if they respect each other's right to be there. Alas, Jeffy contends that this is his corner. Again and again Bonnie tries to slip in beside him. He bites at her head and neck and she runs out to escape. Then she tries to back in. He bites her hip and tail, chasing her out into the wind with a parting snap before he withdraws into the windless comfort of his patio. I do not really think that he plans to chase her out but only that he cannot leave her alone if she is within reach. Poor Bonnie! As I cleaned the stalls, I could hear them surging back and forth. They were at least getting a little excitement and a little exercise before I brought them into their stalls to doze out the rest of the storm.

About a month ago I turned them out together for the first time since Jeffy was weaned, nearly two years ago. I had Bonnie's shoes removed until I saw, at the end of a week, that she would not kick even when cornered. Now she is shod with caulks for winter. At first she avoided Jeffy by quiet and patient movements. Even now she does not want to be cornered by him if she can help it. For example, she never goes into his stall even though it stands open to the paddock with hay and water within. She always lets him precede her through doors when I whistle them in. His biting and worrying of her are, I think, just the pestiferous playfulness of a young animal, not the remnants of his stallion nature. She too will play, but very rarely. Then they look very fierce, as with ears plastered back against their heads and with gleaming teeth they run at each other, only to wheel and kick and plunge at a good, safe distance.

I strung an electric wire all along the cedar fence of the pasture and paddock to stop Jeffy from reaching through to graze outside. He has worn his mane to tatters doing this. Now I hope that it will grow out so that I can show him next summer. He learned this trick when he was a baby. As he grew he got his head painfully stuck several times, but there are still places where he can wiggle it through. Bonnie doesn't even try.

It has been a great satisfaction to help one of my competitors at the gymkhana to train his horse to jump. This mare's attitude to jumping was so reluctant that she had gone at one of the jumps tail first and knocked it down with her hips. Obviously the mare's approach to jumping was all wrong. The first thing we did was to switch from a curb bit to a snaffle and from a western to an English saddle. The next was to try to teach her that a barrier was something to get over at a walk, trot, or canter by paying attention to it, watching where she put her feet, and keeping calm. First we led her at a walk over four heavy poles laid on the ground and wedged in the holes of cinder blocks. Then she was ridden at a walk and a trot over these. At first with her head in the air and her nerves on end, she crashed into almost all of them. She was hugged and stroked if she cleared them. She seemed to learn very quickly that cracking her feet or legs on these poles resulted from her own carelessness. By the second lesson she was clearing them cleanly. Then the poles, still heavily weighted in the cinder blocks, were very gradually raised, the jump course varied, and different types of jumps introduced. In about nine periods of fifteen to thirty

93

minutes over a three-week span, she was jumping a little over two feet cleanly with no refusal or run-out in the whole period. She is now well on her way to win over small jumps in informal gymkhanas like the one where she disgraced herself so badly, due merely to lack of proper training. The ground then froze hard, and since I do not believe in jumping on frozen ground, we will have to wait until next spring.

I cannot understand why so many young people seem to think that flat saddle riding is sissy stuff. Except for rodeo and cattle work, isn't all the fastest and riskiest riding done in flat saddles—racing, polo, hunting, and jumping? I have absolutely nothing against western riding when done correctly. In fact, the western saddle is perfect for the purpose of working cattle and range riding.

Jeffy is still doing well under saddle. I am riding him out around our land almost entirely now because he was beginning to sour on ring work. However, I am glad that I stayed in the ring as long as I did. The drills there on his responses to the aids have very definitely paid off, as shown by the fact that he almost always takes the canter lead I call for and usually straightens out very promptly from a swerving shy on signal from my leg and hand. I have ridden him on the road only a little so far. First, because I feel that at this stage in his education, it is most important to instill good habits of obedience and, second, because he is not shod.

A few days ago, I rode him with Marion and Red. This was his first time in company. Except for the fact that he plastered himself along Red's side, he was as good as gold. Red is perfect for this purpose because he will never kick and because his bold, free walk and trot should serve as a good example to Jeffy.

Jeffy missed nothing on this trip. With his tiny ears and big eyes he questioned every odd-shaped bush, fallen tree, or looming rock. He paid no attention to the cars that passed, although Red jumped at them a few times. Jeffy does shy and even whirl with great suddenness but so all in one piece, so to speak, that so far I have been able to stay with him easily.

I was a little concerned about his trot. It is like a little mo-

torboat, put-put-put, all up and down and not much forward. My textbook tells me, however, that it takes a while
for these youngsters to learn to extend the trot under saddle.
His canter is divine. Bonnie's canter is very irregular, smooth
enough when she sees a jump before her but jarring my
every bone when she puts on one of her passive-resistance
acts against ring work.

In driving I reeducated Jeffy to the point of pulling a log.
The first time I hitched him to this he remembered the fright
of his runaway and would surely have gone again, but I was
leading him with the chain over his nose instead of driving
him with the lines to the bit. We took first one step, then a
few more, and finally a small circle around the paddock,
stopping between each movement for reassurance and calming. The next day I still led him, but this time we went
around the bigger pasture. By the third lesson he was all
over his complex and I could drive him. Since then I have
driven him on foot around the place here, but I still have a
lead line running to his nose just in case of need. This much
I did alone, but I will certainly get help before I hitch him to
the cart again.

CHAPTER 24

Winter

TODAY is Wednesday, February 2, 1955, a dismal gray morning with snow on the ground. The thermometer reads seven degrees. It is nine-thirty and the horses are still in the stable. As a member of the Ground Observer Corps I spot planes on Wednesdays from six to eight, so their breakfast routine is upset. When I leave at about a quarter of six, it is too early for their breakfast and when I return it is too late. They can hear me in the garage next to their stable, and even though it is still black as pitch, they expect room service at once. I usually give them their hay before I leave and grain them on my return. Today I overslept and they had to wait until I got back.

Our earlier snowfall turned out to be a flurry, but yesterday's gave us a couple of inches. It is very late in the year for us to have the first snow deep enough to track a cat. Even this small amount is better than none for the sun-scorched, parched roots of the hay and pasture grass. It has been a bad winter for the land. The loss of good topsoil in the blowing dust and the nuisance of the dust itself points out the need for more winter cover crops. We have no bare land here, but about five acres were reseeded for hay last summer, and the new young plants cannot entirely hold the soil against the prevalent strong west winds.

Because the earth has been so dry and hard, I have started to rub that black, tarry preparation around the coronary bands and heels of my horses' feet. Lanolin is said to be at

96

least as good, but I do not care for the feel of it and Bonnie objects strongly to the smell.

Last year I derived satisfaction with the so-called English winter caulks. I can now report that I used the same set of shoes with the same set of caulks all last winter and, since October, this winter. The shoes are, naturally, reset several times each winter so that the growth of the hoof can be trimmed down. On all feet the two hind caulks are perfectly good; one or two of the front caulks on each shoe are worn down. The remaining seem to prevent slipping very well on the occasional patches of ice on our bare roads this winter. There was very little snow last winter also, so I find the durability of the caulks truly remarkable.

Yesterday a friend and I hitched Jeffy to a toboggan for the first time in his life. He paid no more attention to it than to the treelet he used to pull a year ago. My reins were not long enough for driving from the toboggan, so we took turns riding while the other drove from the ground. I had the longe line on also for insurance but did not have to use it. This, then, was the next step in his rehabilitation as a harness horse.

One of my readers once told me that she thought Jeffy was an imaginary horse. Indeed he is not. He is a very real little Morgan colt, now technically a three-year-old but actually two years and eight months old. Toby and I measured him today. He stands fifteen hands and a half inch and is a very solid, blocky little rich bay with a black mane, tail, and legs.

He wears a halter under his snaffle bridle. This is because he is a little resistant to bitting, so I hold the halter with one hand, and I can easily slip the bit in his mouth without a scene about it. This resistance started one day when I tried to bridle him immediately after a tooth fell out. His gum must have been sore because he would have none of it, although he never caused any trouble before. For the next three days, I dipped the previously moistened bit in granulated sugar. That helped greatly but he is still a little reluctant. Rather than make an issue of the business, I will just keep the halter on until the last trace of resistance goes, as it has almost entirely now. The fact that the arrangement looks rather messy is not important.

I find that little troublesome matters like this evaporate in time, if ignored. Rather than nag and nag at him about something, I prefer to ignore it unless it is serious and he knows that he is wrong; then I may punish him. Just a few days ago this happened. For his whole life he has had his feet handled many times a week, both by me and by the blacksmith. Recently he has taken it into his head that he is no longer going to cooperate. So he shifts about and tries to pull his leg away. Using the ignoring principle I paid no attention and just held on, knowing that this phase would pass eventually. However, when Jeffy actually tried to kick as I cleaned a hind hoof, he went too far. Jeffy knows that he should stand quietly to have his feet handled, and he knows very well that he must never kick. The minute he did so, I reached for a whip that hangs close by and belted him hard just once. Then I picked up the same foot and held it; he was quiet so I praised him. Then I went around and around and handled all four feet over and over again. He is a reformed character in that regard.

The day before yesterday I had a lovely ride on both horses. It was well below freezing with a stiff wind. I didn't get started until three and so only had time for about a half hour on each horse. Jeffy was very gay and lively and had to get a couple of bucks and a jump out of his system before he settled down for training. I was so pleased to find that he is getting the extended trot. I jogged him for twenty steps or so and then the lightest squeeze of my legs would send him on, a slight restraint on my hand would bring him back, and then repeat, all quite smooth and soft for such a young colt. This is a much used exercise for the body and mind of a horse, as both Littauer and Chamberlain write. Physically it supples the body lengthwise, but it also teaches smooth and prompt responses to the rider's leg and hand. The repertoire of a horse longer in training would include such movements as slow walk, extended walk, slow walk, halt, back, slow trot, extended trot, slow trot, halt, back, canter, hand gallop, canter, walk, halt, and so on going up and down the scales of the gaits and their speeds, with or without skipping some of the slower gaits. These exercises cannot be used more than a short time without causing souring. I was very interested to see that Jeffy got it first at the trot. To get an extended walk from a slow walk at my command will be harder, and the halt is far from good now because I am trying to do it with the least possible use of my hand.

When Bonnie's turn came we went through a much more extended pattern of this exercise including the halt, back, and then at once into a canter without any walking steps. She is pretty good at these exercises, but I do not have the skill and I have not taken the time to get as much from her as another could. The aim is not so much the movements themselves but, through your own riding and the horse's training, to do them so smoothly that the use of the aids is practically invisible. However, even with me aboard, training such as this has vastly improved her as a pleasure horse.

Then we worked on the hand-gallop. As anyone who has seen Bonnie jump knows, her pace is too slow. So on the long grassy lane toward home, I pushed her on. In the cold winter air, she really went. She seemed to come unstuck. In rhythm to her stride she blew long ringing snorts—a lovely noise and a wonderful feel. However, alas, I fear the minute we enter a ring, even with jumps in it, she'll get tied up again. I think she has a complex on any kind of ring work.

CHAPTER 25

⁂

March Wind and Mud

MARCH is traditionally the month of wind. Yes, it is that, but to me it is even more the month of mud—fetlock-deep mud, squelchy black mud everywhere. The horses are plastered in mud from poll to tail, at first wet then drying to a ceramic shell. Outdoors as they walk they pierce great holes in the worn-out turf. If they run they slip, cutting long rips in the skin of the earth. Underground freshets undermine the surface, and big holes and fissures appear in what had been solid ground. The horses get wise to these traps for their feet and are careful, even in their play.

Indoors, big fluffs of horsehair roll along the floor, and clouds of dust billow through the air and get in my lungs and in my hair as I try to groom Bonnie and Jeffy into a condition of reasonable presentability. This is the worst season of the year for the owner-groom in the pleasure horse stable. Although seldom a day goes by in winter when the horses are not turned out for a little while at least, this March had our worst weather of the winter. Freezing rain, a sheet of ice, or severe winds have kept them in more days this month than I can remember for all the rest of the winter together.

The grass of the pasture still looks brown and dead, but I can tell by the color of the horses' droppings, which have changed from the yellowish brown of the grain- and hay-fed animal to the very dark brown of the animal on grass, that the new grass is starting to come in. In the course of hours of grazing, the horses manage to collect enough of the tiny new shoots to bring about this change. If I look very closely at the dead old grass of the pasture I can see these tender little blades coming through. This is the time of year to shut the horses out of the pasture to save it from their trampling. However, this is when we go south and leave the horses in young Bill's care. Since they are not exercised, I sacrifice the pasture to them so they may have more liberty than the paddock allows. When I get back in April, I will cut off half the pasture with an electric fence and fertilize it, keeping the horses out until the grass is well up, and then treat the other half. This system worked very well last year.

This is the horses' holiday time. To taper off their exercise, I longed them or rode them a few times. I also took off Bonnie's shoes. Bonnie is shod all year except for this period of about one month. I think it is good for her feet, especially in the mud season. At first she steps short and warily, as I would do on a shale beach. I do not know if this is real tenderness or just a consciousness of how queer her feet feel without shoes. It wears off after a while and she moves naturally.

Except for one six-week period last summer, Jeffy has been barefoot all his life. He will be shod for the life of work of a grown-up horse when we return. I am very proud of his feet. Their conformation is apparently perfect—the front feet round, the hind a little more oval, both with open heels, well-developed frogs, set in a concave sole. With all the riding I did all winter on frozen ground and bare roads there has been little wear and no cracking of the hooves. Regularly, at about six-week intervals, a very fine blacksmith comes to pare them and round the edges of the walls; at the same time he resets Bonnie's shoes.

I have had no leg or foot troubles of any kind with Jeffy. He gets supplementary minerals and he has a legume-rich hay. I have had trouble with Bonnie's feet; they used to tend to dry out and heat, especially in the summer, although last summer I had no trouble. I gave her this barefoot holiday in the mud season last year and also used leathers with tar and oakum in front for the hard dry period of the year. I used a hoof dressing, and lastly I cut out corn entirely from her hot-weather diet. Whether this last had any effect, I don't know. In any case her feet were no problem last year.

As Bonnie gets older she gets better and better in all ways. As a youngster, she had a tendency to puffiness about the hocks and fetlocks, which used to worry me. That seems to be almost gone, despite the fact that I use her harder and trained her to jump and jumped her. She is approaching her eighth birthday, and she is more horse each year.

On March first I introduced Jeffy to the Weymouth bridle in preparation for the show season. For short periods on three consecutive days I bridled him with the two bits without the curb chain and left him in his stall, with some hay, to get used to the feel of so much steel in his mouth. I was very sure there was nothing he could catch the rings on and kept an eye on him. At first he tried everything he could think of to dislodge the bits. The hay helped to take his mind off that effort. By the third day, he accepted them as a matter of course. After that, still without the curb chain and the curb rein unused, I rode him. On my return, I will pick up from there and work on his training more regularly, almost every day if possible.

The other measure I took with the show season in mind was to train his mane to lie over on the off side. It naturally fell on the near side, which is where western horses wear their manes to get them out of the way of the throw of the rope, at least by a right-handed rider. Training the mane is very easy. I first tried to clean down to the roots of the hair with a stiff brush dipped in water. Then I rubbed in a little olive oil, since I noticed he seemed to have an irritation there, and braided it in about twelve little pigtails down the off side of his neck. Fastening the pigtails with rubber bands, I left them thus for about a week. The mane now falls correctly, although I may have to repeat this procedure later.

CHAPTER 26

Some Spring Problems

TODAY I was trying to teach Bonnie the flying change of lead. Last fall she was getting it, but this spring both of us are a little rusty. The trouble is that it requires such perfect timing on my part in relation to her stride. The signal must be given at exactly the right moment in the rhythm of the canter; it is more a matter of training myself than training her. A top-notch horseman, it is said, can tell exactly which leg a horse is moving at any time at all paces. I'm not that good, are you? She got fed up and dumped me as clean as a whistle. She snatched her head out of my hands, put it between her legs, lifted her rear into the air, and tossed me very neatly. Since I had my usual grip on the reins, she got quite a jab on the mouth. I was pleased to see that after that episode she made the next two changes very nicely without even one of her ladylike bucks so frequent at the canter-depart.

She's a funny girl. Maybe it is because she is a mare that she has these flares of temper. Most of the time she is as quiet and good and reliable as a horse can be, but she can blow up. Under trail-riding conditions in large companies of horses she is one seething cauldron of upset emotions. Sometimes she is much worse than at other times, which may be connected with her periods of heat. She doesn't want horses coming up behind her. She doesn't want them in front of her. She doesn't know what she wants and neither do I. She will get a crush on another horse and be an angel as long as we ride together and a torment if we separate.

103

Once it was a big bay ex-cavalry horse of unknown parentage and once it was a Morgan stallion. She had met neither before, nor had I met their riders. She loves her Amherst friend, Red, and all is well as long as we go together, but I have to find her another boyfriend fast if he leaves her. The upshot is that neither of us cares at all for group rides. I do hope Jeffy will be better in this respect, and since he is a gelding I think there is a better chance. Yesterday I rode him with two others and he was very good.

Jeffy was no trouble at all about his second shoeing. Last year at about this time he was shod for a six-week period. So it has been almost a year since he was shod. I eased him up to it by handling his feet a lot and tapping the edges of his hooves with the metal handle of the hoof pick to accustom him to the little blows and bangs of nailing. I want my horses to behave for the blacksmith, who is top-notch. I don't want him to have to use up his strength and mind training my horses or fighting their bad manners. I was proud of Jeffy. He was a good boy.

I am trying to exercise them both almost every day, even if only for half an hour. This is where the owner who uses professional help has it over us owner-trainer-grooms. A rigid and regular routine can give the former a good edge over the self-help showman, whose other duties and interests demand his or her time. A housewife and clubwoman like myself has guests, parties, civic duties, club duties, and all the things that go into running a house and a garden. The amateur horseman usually has a business demanding regular hours, and he too has civic and social duties. No, I am seldom surprised when the professionally cared for and trained horse wins over the amateur's. This is quite apart from technical know-how, which to be sure is usually but not always superior. Regularity of feeding, grooming, and the planning and routine execution of a training schedule does tend to give such horses that extra polish that can put them at the top.

The obvious question is—why do I bother to show at all? The sheer physical effort of fitting to show is severe. I loathe moving the horses around in a trailer. However, there is nothing like a show to give an incentive for some real work on my own horsemanship and on my horses' training and condition. Both I and my horses are far better because I plan to show. Actually, I show very little. The one show I wouldn't miss for anything is, of course, our own National Morgan Horse Show. I should force myself to show Jeffy elsewhere before then. Afterward I'll probably do one or two small local shows.

To plan to enter the 100-mile ride would have the same effect on my outlay of time and thought, but that does not appeal to me. I happen to prefer the short rides with the emphasis on training to the long hours with the emphasis on conditioning. Other folks have a perfect right to feel otherwise. Of course, a person who does not need the incentive of competition to meet goals can achieve all this staying peacefully at home.

When we got back from our vacation the pasture looked frightful, all torn up by hooves on soggy, wet land. I made a little temporary pasture in the lane, approximately 300 feet by 30 feet, which runs between the pasture and our multiflora rosebush boundary. This five-year-old hedge is almost tight enough to hold the horses, but it is shaded at one point by two cherry trees on our neighbor's land. There gaps exist, so I strung an electric wire along it for insurance. Then I cut the horses out of their proper pasture, fertilized the acre with 600 pounds of 10-10-10 lawn fertilizer, and let it grow for a month. It is now very lush and for a few days I won't dare to let them in for more than a half hour, gradually increasing it.

My horses are plagued with pinworms this spring. Veterinarians seem to have very little interest in these rectal worms. I read many books on horse care but find almost no attention paid to these worms. I remember an hour talk on parasites in horses without one mention of pinworms. I have asked three veterinarians for advice or, better yet, to come out and treat them for these worms. My best answer was from the great Doc who told me to get some quassia chips from any drugstore, make a solution from them, and administer rectally. I won't go into further details because I am no authority on medicating horses and I wouldn't want you to try and follow my methods. Anyway, I did so and the horses are still alive and I think the pinworms are gone, unless they are just building up their population. I would appreciate it if someone would write a comprehensive article on the life cycle and control of the pinworm. They may not be very injurious, but they surely are annoying. Of all the worms they are the most obvious to us poor amateur owner-grooms, so I think they deserve more attention from the medical profession.

CHAPTER 27

Jeffy Goes to College

I THOUGHT of sending Jeffy to college. I did so. On the very field where a long time ago I shot arrows into the air because the college doctor would not allow me to do anything more strenuous for physical education, young Jeffy took a ten-day short course in how to be a good saddle horse. This is probably one of the shortest training periods under professional tuition that a would-be show horse ever had. It had to be that short because his teacher, Mr. Nichols, had his stalls full before then and left for the North with his horses after that. The aim was to get the happy-go-lucky, easygoing young Jeffy to realize that life is not all beer and skittles, to get up on his toes, into his bit, and fight for the good old blue.

Why did I choose Mr. Nichols? To be sure his stable is near. However, that is not really important since I stayed away from Jeffy as much as if he had been miles away. I did not really want a last-minute cram course for showing. I hoped that these ten days would give me a good-going pleasure horse that knew how to get into his bit, pick up his feet, and work in a ring if called on to do so. Mr. Nichols is a man who has trained a great variety of horses—in harness, for flat racing, for hunter hack, American saddle bred for show, and school horses for teaching. He is a lightweight man, and he is a good man with a horse. I have known him for quite a few years and had no hesitation about leaving Jeffy with him and with the girls who help him.

He worked Jeffy briefly every day, usually in the cool of

the evening. With his legs, his voice, and the swish and crack of a whip he urged him into his bit. He worked him much more up and down the straight sides of his ring than around and around. Even with a true-moving horse like Jeffy, going around and around can get him hopping on the turns. For at least the first eight days, Mr. Nichols would not canter him at all, saying that the trot must be established first. At first Jeffy sweated very heavily, and they had to walk him after workouts. By the end of the ten days he was much harder. I had cut his grazing before he went but not enough, and my own almost daily workouts were apparently not strenuous enough to really harden him for these intensive lessons.

I remember Jeffy at the trot a few days before he went to college. When he came home I almost did not recognize him as the same horse. Before college he was very relaxed, trotting along like a quiet little child's horse and rather sleepy about it. After college he was up on his toes, with head and tail in the air looking as if he could give you a really good ride. That tells the story. He is a far better pleasure horse because of those ten days than he ever was before. He goes into the bit, and he picks up his feet. He carries you as if it was a job, but one he enjoys. I do think, although I do not intend to boast, that Mr. Nichols did not have to cope with any really bad habits that I had unwittingly taught, except Jeffy's basic easygoingness. His head carriage was good, I was told, and he had no vices whatsoever.

One often hears that professional training may make a horse hard to handle for an amateur. Maybe this is occasionally true of training for showing specifically. However, it was certainly not true in Jeffy's case. When he came home he was pretty keyed up for a couple of days and jumped around in his stall more than he ever has before. The minute his saddle and bridle were on, however, he calmed right down and was not a whit harder to ride than he had been before. He still stood like a rock to mount and dismount. In fact, he is better, since he is less likely to try and get his head down for a buck or two. So many thanks Mr. Nichols, you certainly accomplished a great deal in ten days. I wish you could have had him longer.

108

So now we come to the show and what happened? Jeffy came down with colic and I scratched him from the saddle classes. Probably it is just as well. For the first week after I had Jeffy back I worked him regularly and hard. We were doing fine. Then for the next two weeks or so, I was so swamped by work for that same show that I had no time to work either horse except in the most sketchy fashion. I put Bonnie over a few jumps and worked on some equitation riders while I sat on Jeffy mostly in the middle of the ring. That is the sort of thing that happens when you try to do everything yourself. So maybe Jeffy's nervous stomach, which couldn't take life on the show grounds, saved us from making monkeys of ourselves in front of thousands of people. However, Jeffy's college education will always be valuable and I am very glad he had it.

George Nichols rides the three-year-old Jeffy, June 1955. Mr. Nichols has got him up and into the bit. Jeffy is light, collected, alert, and animated.

CHAPTER 28

Talking

I CAN remember how surprised I was when a well-known authority on the management of horses remarked during his talk at a meeting that he could tell if his horses had been well cared for by their silence when he came into the stable in the evening. Of course, that is quite true, but it surprised me because we one- and two-horse owners tend to sentimentalize our relations with our horses and visualize them as greeting and fawning on us like dogs. Actually, mine do not do this any more than his do. Of course there may be exceptions, especially among horses who live alone. As I see them around here, and thinking back to the time when Bonnie was my only horse, horses who live alone are very lonesome and grateful for the slightest kind attention. However, horses stabled with their own kind or with a dog, goat, or other animal tend on the whole to be pretty self-sufficient, socially speaking.

I thought of the professor's remark as I drove into the garage late one night after an absence of some days. Our stable is the other half of the garage, separated from the cars by a wall and a door. So deep was the silence even after I opened the door into the stable that my heart stopped with the fear that Bonnie and Jeffy were gone. I turned on the light and two sets of serene and solemn eyes were watching me over the stall partitions. I looked in the stalls and found full water pails and hay left from dinner, clean stalls and clean horses, and swept aisles. Thanks to young Bill, my horses were clean and content, with no reason to speak to me when I came in.

In contrast to this picture of silent contented horses, I'll tell you of another incident. A few weeks ago I went to visit a poor old horse that leads a very rough life. This horse will usually have nothing to do with man, if he can help it. He is hard to approach when you go into his pen. I was very much surprised and at first pleased to have him come right up to me, talking and breathing on me softly. Well, what a nice change! Then I looked about me. The floor was filthy and so was the horse. There was water, but there was not a speck of bedding or food anywhere. I went up into the hayloft, and there was no hay. I looked in the grain bin and saw only an empty bag. That poor horse was telling me he was terribly hungry. He was so hungry he no longer feared man! So when my horses talk to me, I ask myself, "What do they want?"

Oh yes, they do talk but not at night because they never go to bed hungry or thirsty. They talk in the daytime, especially Bonnie, for several reasons. First, because they think it must be time for grain, even if they are an hour or so early. Second, because for some reason I have not turned them out; perhaps it is raining very hard or there is a sheet of ice outside. Right now they are upset because I have cut them out of the pasture, which is being plowed. Now and then they will talk because they are bored and want to be up and doing, but this was much more common when Bonnie lived alone.

It was almost a year after I first bought her before Bonnie would condescend to speak to me. Now she is very expressive. She does not mutter softly and affectionately but she calls her demands piercingly. If she wants to go out she lays back her ears and shakes her head, then cocks her ears to see if I am catching her meaning. Jeffy has not got the hang of self-expression yet, but he will mutter when he sees me pick up the grain measure. Instead of shaking his head to indicate his impatience to go out, he bounces up and down in his stall—not so much to communicate his meaning, as Bonnie does, but just from happy anticipation that I may open his door to freedom.

They talk to each other a good deal. When Jeffy was still a stallion he used that soft urgent grunting, which is stud talk, to both Bonnie and me. That continued for many months after gelding but is gone now. When I turn them out together they greet each other with soft mutterings. They call ringingly when I take one out of sight of the other. Now and then Bonnie gives the mare squeal that threatens Jeffy with a kick.

I speak of the pasture being plowed. It was a horrible sight in August. In some places it seemed to grow straight ragweed. The horses would come in with their faces and nostrils yellow with pollen. Aside from poverty of grass, it was loaded with parasites. I had both horses checked for worms last week. They are free of both blood- and stomach worms, but they have a good crop of pinworms.

If I were to have the acre pasture seeded to grass this fall, I am told I should keep the horses off until it is well up next spring. That was too depressing a thought. I like to turn them out for a while each day all winter and the paddock is only fifty by eighty feet, not big enough for proper exercise, or so I think. They are used to the larger area and would miss it. The farmer who will do it suggested I seed the pasture, after thorough plowing and harrowing, to winter rye, which they could run on all winter after it was up a ways this fall. Then next spring it may be possible just to harrow the rye and seed the permanent grasses right into it. However, it remains to be seen whether or not a second plowing will be needed.

CHAPTER 29

~~~~~~

More on Showing
and Safety

EARLIER I wrote that I had a slippery smooth cement floor in my barn. I applied asphalt roofing paper to the cement of the aisle to reduce slipping by the horses. I got this idea from a large training stable and breeding farm where I had seen it used for this purpose.

I can now report, after about six weeks' use, that I find it completely satisfactory, and what a pleasure it is to lead the horses in over it with free bold strides or just let them come into the barn loose from the pasture. Heretofore, they walked in with little careful steps, or if they got absent-minded at least one leg would slither out from under. My aisle is L shaped with the saddling and grooming area near the door and, at right angles to that, the passage between the stalls. I did the grooming area first as an experiment. They moved so freely there that they became careless about the passage. Bonnie did a split and Jeffy went down so far that he nearly bumped both stifles. I did the second branch of the L in a hurry after that.

I laid the paper myself, and this is how I did it. I got the heaviest of the roofing papers. It comes in three-foot widths. This meant I had to use two widths in the grooming area and a width and a half in the stall passage. I unrolled a length of coils and promptly fell over the hidden roll, skinning both knees. The first strip I battened down to the wooden sill, but I later found that it was unnecessary with the waterproof linoleum adhesive I used.

In the first area I put the adhesive under all the paper. In the second strip I spread the adhesive just along the edges and at the ends. I did not want the paper to go scooting under the horses like a scatter rug. The hardware store clerk told me I should roll the paper over the adhesive with a weighted roller. Since we didn't have one I just pressed with my feet to squeeze the surplus adhesive out toward the edge and then anchored the ends with rocks for a couple of hours. I do have a few blisters under it where the air is trapped. There probably are better adhesives. A can of something comes with the paper and a lot of nails. Obviously, I couldn't use the nails on a cement floor and the can didn't have any directions on it; so I got this waterproof linoleum cement complete with directions. I had to have a spreader, which is a little toothed gadget, and some wood alcohol to clean the nasty brown mess off myself when I was through. To cut the paper I found that the best thing was one of those wicked sharp asparagus knives that feed stores sell cheaply.

I confess that I have a horrid nagging fear that when the paper eventually wears out in patches I won't be able to un-stick the rest of it to expose the floor smoothly for a new layer. If you are thinking of trying this flooring I suggest you do a little more research on it than I did. For example, Toby would have been more pleased with me if I had asked him to plane down the bottom of the tack room door before I laid the paper, instead of afterward. He had an awful time get-ting at the hinges.

Little Jeffy is in fine shape. He made his debut in an open Morgan class two weeks ago and placed third right after two old, seasoned show-ring performers. To be sure I tried to keep him behind his mother and he was going great guns into his bit trying to catch up with her. Since I was holding him back, naturally we put on quite a show of action and animation. When I told Mr. Nichols, his college professor, about this he had a good laugh. Ah well, was that not show-manship? To give Jeffy full credit, I did pass Bonnie at the trot and the canter and he kept on going just as well. Dear old Bonnie herself picked up the pleasure Morgan blue and the open trail horse red and a third in equitation, so we were all very happy on the long haul home.

Bonnie and I are certainly a case of if at first you don't succeed, try, try again. For the first three years of our small-scale showing we were lucky to pick up a low ribbon. She is nine this year and this is her big year. We have made five shows, ranging from the National Morgan Horse Show to a tiny gymkhana-show combination. She picked up ten blues in pleasure-type or equitation classes and only once failed to gain ribbons in the classes she didn't win (that was in this open Morgan saddle class in which she served as Jeffy's bait). I say this to give the good girl credit, to boast a little, and I hope to encourage some of you. I know what it is like to hear those numbers called off for the ribbons and yours is not among them.

If your horse is young, bear in mind that his body will not fully develop until he is about six. I firmly believe you cannot expect good consistent performance and top looks without maturity. It would be a mistake to rush him. This does not include in-hand classes, of course, for young age groups. So keep trying. Obviously your horse must be sound and a reasonably good one in the first place. He should be sleek, well muscled, and thoroughly schooled.

Both of you need to know the technique of the job of showing. A long time ago I learned that I have to know what my horse can do, in other words, what classes to put her in. Unless it is a tiny show, I do not put her in an open Morgan park performance class. She is not that kind of Morgan. She is a pleasure and trail Morgan, so those are the classes I put her in. Young Jeffy is still an unknown in his capabilities. At present I choose the open Morgan because he is more showy than Bonnie and not trained well enough for pleasure, loose-rein classes.

CHAPTER 30

Better and Better
Each Year

O NE of my readers wrote that she had recently obtained a three-year-old Morgan that had been trained to drive and started under saddle and she wanted to finish him herself. She is finding that while ridden he holds his head rather low and asked if I used a bitting harness on Jeffy or, if not, in what way a satisfactory head carriage developed.

She understands that young horses do tend to be low headed in their early saddle education. This is my understanding, too, for the majority at least. It was very true with my own two. Apparently, it is related to the fact that the unaccustomed weight of the rider, especially on young muscles, throws off the natural balance of the horse. It shifts the center of gravity, which in the free horse lies about back of the withers, forward. In the course of time, varying from a few months to a year, the horse will regain its normal balance with the rider in the saddle, greatly assisted by muscles strengthened through exercise. Thus, in time, the horse will hold its head in a position to its conformation, if the rider does not interfere too much with its head. She does not mention it, but I bet that the youngster at this stage also trips over anything in a most distressing manner.

Nature then, plus judicious riding, will help to get that head up to the level natural to that particular horse. Now, of course, we all know that any Morgan can do anything, maybe. However, it is just as well to recognize that some horses of a breed are naturally more of a peacock and others more of a using kind. Neither one is better than the other. Goodness is a matter of soundness, conformation, disposition, and way of going, so either kind of horse can be good or bad.

If this three-year-old is a peacock and if his owner wishes to campaign seriously when he is older in the open Morgan classes, as distinct from the Morgan pleasure classes, she will probably want to cultivate further the high natural head carriage by much work in the bitting harness with almost all riding done in show form within a ring or on a smooth straightaway. That is the sort of training the professionally handled horse would get for a show-ring career. One trainer, I am told, had a Morgan he planned to show under saddle, and he did almost all his exercising in harness. The harness work gives results very similar to a bitting harness and is more interesting, probably, to both the horse and the trainer. Obviously the horse was already well trained for showing under saddle.

Even if your colt is a peacock, you certainly don't have to make him such a specialist if you are not interested in a purely show career. Few of us one- or two-horse owners want to keep to such a dull routine with our pride and joy. However, if we don't, we should not complain when we are beaten in the peacock classes.

So now for the using horse. There is certainly no reason why you can't use the above routine to make him more of a peacock, if that is where your interest lies. Bear in mind it will be tedious. On the other hand, you may want to produce a really nice pleasure horse for your daily enjoyment. As far as I can make out, a little work in the bitting harness does no harm. As I remember back, I used a bitting harness on Jeffy for about two weeks or a month off and on. Jeffy was about a year or eighteen months old, just before we started to drive. I think the point was not so much to set the head as to illustrate to him the futility of fighting the bit.

Last night I met Mr. Nichols. He said he was getting a half brother to Jeffy to train next week and that he had sent over a bitting harness to the owners, so they could give him a little bitting before he came to start serious saddle training as a pleasure horse. When he had Jeffy he told me distinctly that Jeffy did not need work in the bitting harness. It must have been because Jeffy and I had gotten beyond that point. He was then three and it had been at least a year since he had had one on and about eight months since I started him under saddle. He did, however, say that the best thing for Jeffy would be lots of driving. This I echo gladly for that age. It muscles up their rears and conditions and strengthens them, without the weight on their still-undeveloped spines.

For the well-schooled pleasure horse, the hunter, the cross-country horse, and the generally using horse, excessive use of a bitting harness has the danger of making them too rigid. You see what I mean? The checkrein prevents a free head-to-tail movement of the muscles along the spine. The side reins from bit to saddle prevent the free lateral movements from side to side. These two flexibilities, lengthwise and sidewise, are terribly important in all riding other than the round the rail of the show horse, where the action with maximum bloom is what counts. They are what other systems try to cultivate in the horse, culminating in dressage work but starting from the same exercises that make the best of all pleasure horses. There is extensive worldwide literature on these systems, with slight variations. To avoid confusion I will name only one book, which is excellent, although hard to find. It is *Training Hunters, Jumpers and Hacks*, by Harry D. Chamberlain. This U.S. Army general was, I suspect, the author of our own old Cavalry manual, which is just about as good if you can find a copy. These systems never use a bitting harness even at the start, although one recommends a dumb-jockey, an artificial aid that is not quite so much of a straitjacket.

[Editor's note to this edition: If any of you want to read up on the subject of dressage, there is a recent book out, *An Illustrated Guide to Dressage* by Jennie Loriston-Clarke.]

Well, I have gotten a long way from that colt with his head down. It appears that in the course of time with careful exercise the head will come up to its normal position with no outside interference. To get it even higher some trainers use hours of work in either a bitting harness or a driving harness with checkrein; others raise it by developing the horse as a muscular and responsive athlete through planned exercises. The writer of the letter asked if the use of a Weymouth following early practice in the snaffle helped to raise Jeffy's. The answer is either no or it ought not to have done so. It is supposed to be the snaffle working in the corner of the lips of the horse that raises the head. The curb should flex the jaw and bring the chin toward the vertical (but not too far). No, Jeffy carries his head the best of all with a snaffle bit and no checkrein in harness. He is naturally somewhat more of a peacock than Bonnie, but sometimes I think I love my using mare, Bonnie, the best. At ten she is more horse than he is, even if he can buck me sky-high as he did yesterday and caught me again before I hit the snow. I want to know him at six and eight and ten, just like I have known her. They get better and better each year.

EPILOGUE

EVENTUALLY Janet moved on to deep involvement in other activities and sold Jeffy. He found his way to another excellent home with the Archibald Cox family, where he happily lived for the last twelve years of his life. As Mrs. Cox said at a recent meeting with Janet and me, "He was truly a part of our family."

Jeffy's temperament was always predictable, except when in harness. Perhaps that was because he had been badly frightened once by an incident right out of the old movies. One day Jeffy was placidly pulling a cart on East Pleasant Street in Amherst, Massachusetts, when he was passed by a pickup truck filled with crates of chickens. One crate slipped off the truck and burst open releasing the chickens. With much squawking and a flurry of feathers, they flew right up toward his face. Poor Jeffy never got over that fright.

Despite his fears when he was driven, Jeffy was calm and collected, even on a busy road, when his rider was astride. He was big for a Morgan, majestic, and had tremendous presence. When Mrs. Cox took him on the road, strangers would stop to ask about him. "He was a wonderful salesman for the Morgan breed!" she exclaimed at our meeting.

In addition to being a pleasure to ride, Jeffy was a dependable winner of ribbons in national-level horse shows. Mrs. Cox recalled, "I don't think he ever came out of the ring without a ribbon. The year my daughter rode him in the National Morgan Horse Show he was the National Grand Champion Gelding. It was all very exciting! We had three award-winning Morgans that year, but Jeffy was the best."

Jeffy was the best in many ways, bringing affection and a mountain of ribbons to his owners. Magnificent in spirit and appearance and living up to the regal qualities of his official name (Lord Jeff), he was the result of both good breeding and skilled training. Janet Wilder Dakin raised only one horse, but she raised a grand champion.

Sheila Rainford